"A wonderfully informative and useful book that will be invaluable to anyone wanting to get started in the movie business. I wish it had been around when I started my career."
–Simon Wincer, (The Phantom; Operation Dumbo Drop; Free Willy; Lonesome Dove)

"Breaking & Entering is an invaluable field guide to surviving the day-to-day rigors of a Hollywood movie set as seen from the unique vantage point of an experienced Production Assistant. Anyone interested in understanding the nuts and bolts of a working film crew will want to read this book."
–Jeffrey Boam, Screenwriter (Lethal Weapon 3; Indiana Jones & The Last Crusade; The Lost Boys)

"Breaking & Entering is the condensed version of what I learned over several shows of pounding the pavement in production. If you want to make it—read it!! . . . and don't forget it."
–Bill Bannerman, Unit Production Manager (Dead Man On Campus; Bridges of Madison County; Unforgiven)

breaking & entering

LAND YOUR FIRST JOB IN
FILM PRODUCTION

april fitzsimmons

BREAKING & ENTERING:
Land Your First Job in Film Production
Copyright © 1997 by April Fitzsimmons

LONE EAGLE PUBLISHING CO.™
1024 N. Orange Drive
Hollywood, CA 90038
Phone 323.308.3400 or 800.815.0503
A division of IFILM^{SM} Corp., www.ifilmpro.com

Printed in the United States of America

Cover design by Lindsay Albert

Library of Congress Cataloging in Publication Data
Fitzsimmons, April,
    Breaking & Entering: Land Your First Job in Film
Production / by April Fitzsimmons
        p.   cm.
    Includes index.
    ISBN 0-943728-91-6
    1. Motion pictures—Production and direction—
Vocational guidance—United States. I. Title.
    PN1995.9.P7F57   1997
    791.43'0232'023—dc21   97-8328
                                            CIP

Contents

PART V

PART VII

Foreword

I began my film career twice: once in 1978 as Roger Corman's Executive Assistant (the better the title, the worse the salary) during his tenure as founder and president of New World Pictures, then again in 1979 when I worked as a production assistant on Roger's feature, *Humanoids From The Deep*. In my second entry-level job, on the set of a feature film, I was hopelessly lost.

Had April Fitzsimmons' book been available then, I would have saved a great deal of wasted time and energy. I wouldn't have made the mistakes most first-timers make on the set.

Breaking & Entering is a truly valuable how-to guide, full of insights and tips from one of the most conscientious and committed people currently working in the film industry. I guarantee that you will learn from her experience if you follow her sage advice.

The motion picture business is a fierce and competitive arena. Forewarned, as they say, is forearmed. And I can think of no better tool to serve you in your quest for a career in production than to read and heed the wisdom provided herein.

Gale Anne Hurd
Producer

Preface

UNION FILMS VERSUS NONUNION FILMS

Starting out in film production as a set production assistant was an excellent learning experience for me. I was afforded many unique opportunities. The stories and experiences shared in this book reflect my personal experiences and are not necessarily the "norm."

If you work on nonunion films, you will have a much more "hands-on" experience. If you work on union films (or films where the Directors Guild of America has jurisdiction), you will be more of an observer. All jobs on union films are strictly defined and off-limits to those not members of the particular union. There are advantages to working on both kinds of projects. I was often given responsibilities on nonunion films that are usually given to DGA trainees or second assistant directors on union films. You may not have the same experiences as you enter the trenches of filmmaking; however, you will be learning about the process regardless of what path you choose. I wish you all the best as you follow your passion.

GENDER BENDER

Both men and women tackle the many jobs involved in film production. Because of this, in *Breaking & Entering*, you will encounter "he," "she," "him" and "her." I did not intend to offend men or women by excluding them from any job category, and if it appears as such—I apologize.

Acknowledgments

Many people contributed encouragement and wisdom to this book. From the production world I would especially like to thank Gale Anne Hurd, Simon Wincer, Alan Ladd, Jr., Jeffrey Boam, Jeff Downer, Marie Cantin, Graham Place, Bill Bannerman, Art Levinson, Jeffrey Wetzel, Jeff Okabayashi, Mary Ellen Woods, Laura Tateishi, Carla Brand Breitner, Terry Miller, John Kretchmer, Jimmy Skotchdopole, Michael Zimbrich, Robert Leveen, Bobby Donaldson, Mike Viglietta, Maggie Murphy, Doug Ornstein, Seth Edelstein, Carole Keligian, Tina Stauffer, Carla Corwin, Simon Warnock, Deb Atkins, Donald Sparks, Jon Scheide, Adam Glickman, Robert Kay, Brad Morris, Dina Brendlinger, Laura Stuart, Candice Campos, Derek Jan Vermaas, Christian Clarke, Tammy Dickson, Stephanie O'Brien, Michael Jefferson, David Waters, Derek Smith, Joanne Guthrie, Bonnie Abaunza, Valerie Flueger, Anne Mitchell, Ed Tapia, David Burr, Peter Collister, David Garden, Jim Rossow, and Jed Mortenson.

I would like to thank my Mom and Dad and my incredible siblings, Brian, Kelly, Julie, Mary and Matt, who have always indulged my crazy ideas.

I would like to thank Joan Singleton and Bethann Wetzel for believing in me and gently guiding me through this process and Jeff Black for his contagious excitement about the project and lastly Blake Busby for his meticulous formatting and design.

Part I

"My first job as a production assistant was on a film called *Humanoids From The Deep*. We were shooting in Northern California and it had rained all day. When the company wrapped at dusk, I was told to stay and help one grip wrap out the entire set. At dawn the next morning, my 24th birthday, we were still there coiling heavy, muddy cable in the pouring rain."

Gale Anne Hurd, Producer
Virus, Dante's Peak, Relic, Aliens,
Terminator II, The Abyss, Terminator

1

The Production Assistant

Breaking & Entering is a book designed to give you a general idea about how to break into production and have a good time along the way. With the proper tools and information, your first steps into film production will be a little easier. Once you are in, the motivation and persistence are up to you. In this book you will find things I wish I'd known before getting started: things I've learned along the way through trial and error, or by people gently guiding me along, making my journey both challenging and rewarding.

YOU ARE WHAT YOU DO

Most production knowledge comes from firsthand experience. Film schools cannot teach you what it's like to work in production. *Breaking & Entering* is PA–101. The rest is up to you.

PRODUCTION TRACK VERSUS
THE DEVELOPMENT TRACK

There are two tracks you can take as a production assistant (PA): development and production. Either channel is entry level and a good place to start. It depends on your long-term goals. The production track is for those who want to work their way up the production ladder. PAs usually end up as ADs, unit production managers, line producers or department heads. The development track deals more with developing projects rather than actual hands-on production. These people work as agents, heads of development, creative executives and studio executives. *Breaking & Entering* deals with the production track and the set PA. Read Hugh Taylor's excellent book, *The Hollywood Job Hunters Survival Guide* (1993, Lone Eagle Publishing), if you are interested in pursuing the development track.

In production there are many types of PAs. There is the office PA, the art department PA, the accounting PA and others. This book is designed for the set PA, but can apply to other types as well. It is a good introduction for anyone who wants to get his or her feet wet.

Your Set Family

Your set family is integral to your survival in this business. These are the people who will nurture you, train you and hopefully carry you with them to their next movie.

FIRST ASSISTANT DIRECTOR (1ST AD)

First ADs run the set and have been in the biz for five to ten years. First ADs have paid their dues, have a history of set experience and basically control the environment of the set. They are the key liaison between the director and the crew, helping the director obtain what he or she wants within the production limits (i.e., time and money). The 1st AD can often set the tone of the show. They generate the schedules and breakdowns and keep the production running smoothly from day to day. They maintain a safe environment on the set by conducting safety meetings. They keep the show on schedule and generate the pace of shooting. They are responsible for directing the background artists or extras.

There are many styles of ADs but mainly they fall into two categories: "The Screamers" and "The Other Ones." The screamers are not much fun, but when you are new you can learn from everyone—good or bad—by keeping an open mind.

First ADs are busy people. Do not get in their way. Be good to them. Try not to bother them too much. Make sure they have everything they need (food, water, etc.) Keep their walkie-talkie batteries charged and a pen nearby. Work with the transportation department to keep their cars clean and full of gas. Maintain a professional

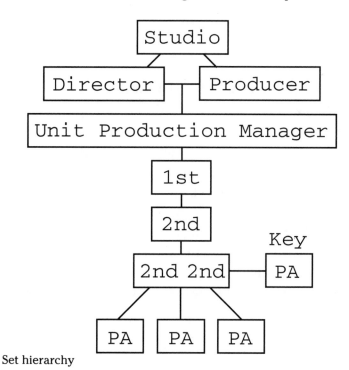

Set hierarchy

attitude. Make their lives easier and, hopefully, they will not forget you.

SECOND ASSISTANT DIRECTOR (KEY 2ND AD)

The Key 2nd AD is one of the hardest working people on the show. To be a 1st AD, you need to pay your dues as a 2nd AD. The 2nd AD answers to everyone. They design and publish the call sheet. They figure out when to bring actors in, when to bring the crew in, when to feed everyone—all the who, the what, the when, the where and the why. They also set most of the background (extras). Although 2nd ADs seem tough and insensitive, do not take it personally. It is the nature of their job. Soon they will be a 1st AD and, perhaps, can relax a little. The 2nd AD can never sleep, sit or complain. They are like army tanks that keep the company steadily moving down the road of completing principal photography.

SECOND SECOND ASSISTANT DIRECTOR (2ND 2ND AD)

On most shows, the 2nd 2nds are in charge of running base camp. They also make sure actors are ready on time. If the actors need anything special, the 2nd 2nd oversees getting it for them. Coordinating with the hair, makeup and wardrobe departments, they figure out the timing of getting the actors ready to shoot. This helps the 2nd AD determine when to bring the actors in to work. On larger productions, it may be necessary to bring in an additional 2nd 2nd to deal with heavy extra days or to work with the picture cars.

PRODUCTION OFFICE

Although the production office is not physically located on the set, you will find yourself working closely with the people in that office. Trust them; communicate with them; rely on them. It will make your life much easier if you can establish a good working relationship with the production office early on.

Entry Level Positions

ASSISTANT DIRECTORS TRAINING PROGRAM

The trainee is part of the Directors Guild of America's Producer Training Plan. They have been handpicked to participate in "AD Boot Camp" and are learning what it takes to be an assistant director. They are trained to prepare the *production report* and call sheet as well as solve problems on the set. Most DGA films will have a trainee.

SET PRODUCTION ASSISTANT (SET PA)

This is the entry level job on a film set and the job that will be discussed in this book. Breaking & Entering is designed to assist anyone entering, or wanting to enter, the business of filmmaking.

Golden Rules

1. The Answer Is Always "Yes"
2. Be Available
3. Respect and Common Courtesy
4. When in Doubt, Ask
5. Have a Sense of Urgency
6. Don't Panic!
7. Don't Be Afraid to Admit You Don't Know Something
8. Don't be Afraid to Admit When You Are Wrong or Have Make a Mistake
9. Don't Be Afraid; It's Only a Movie
10. Have Fun!

2

The Production Assistant's Golden Rules

On most sets, you will find yourself ahead of the game if you can follow The Golden Rules. Feel free to add any of your own.

Explaining the Rules

THE ANSWER IS ALWAYS "YES"

It may sound extreme, but it is the answer that works most often. Your job as a production assistant is to facilitate, communicate and help people get from Point A to Point B. Even if you do not know the answer—make it *seem* as if you are capable of finding the answer. This shows that you can think on your feet and are not afraid of a little challenge. Nothing is more frustrating to a 1st AD than to hear a PA mumble and elaborate why she cannot turn on the air conditioning. She should say she is doing her best to handle it, or she is working on it, or . . .YES! No Problem. This is all anyone wants to hear when they are trying to accomplish many tasks at once. YES.

BE AVAILABLE

Hang around the set . . . not too close, just close enough so the ADs can see you if they need you. Try not to chitchat with the other crew members for too long. Then you become unavailable. Being available means putting yourself where the action is—out of the way—in order to *facilitate*. Sometimes it's not where the action is, sometimes it means being perched on the top of a hill holding a radio in the air so there is a decent radio signal. Being available can also mean helping when you see the crew move into a *new deal* or a new setup (each time the camera changes positions). Sometimes it's as simple as getting water or coffee for someone who looks as if they need it. Be aware of your surroundings.

RESPECT AND COMMON COURTESY

If you want to get along with the crew, you need to respect their positions. You should understand that most people standing around you have done at least ten movies and some have done more than 100. Good movie crew members have a great deal of experience. People do not get hired again if they are not good at what they do. If someone snaps at you, do not take it personally. Most of the time it's all about the work. They are under the gun or have just been snapped at. Respect everyone's gear. Everyone has their little space on the set. To do something quickly you might put your drink on the camera gear (a no-no), or borrow a roll of tape from the grips and forget to return it. Respect the people and their stuff. Avoid the vicious rumor mill. If you cannot say something nice, it's better not to say anything at all. Someday, you may need a job from that person. It's a small community. Use your "pleases" and "thank yous" (and some reliable deodorant).

WHEN IN DOUBT, ASK

If you do not know the answer, ask—preferably the 2nd 2nd AD or another PA. It will save much time and embarrassment. Everyone has been where you are. Sometimes they forget, but they have been there. Admit that you do not know where the bathrooms are . . . but you are going to find out. Try to ask people in person rather than going on the radio and admitting to everyone that you have absolutely NO idea where the 300 box lunches are! It's *always* better to ask than run around in circles.

HAVE A SENSE OF URGENCY

On a film set, time *is* money. Whatever you are doing—however mundane—do not look bored. Stay alert and pay attention to what is going on around you. Not only will you learn a great deal, but people will start to rely on you more. Once the crew recognizes that you seem to know what the scene order is for the day and who is required in the next scene, you will become an asset. Be a self starter. If you see someone struggling with a big heavy box—open the door! One of the biggest complaints I hear from ADs is, "My PA has no sense of urgency." This means the PA takes her own sweet time doing whatever it is she has been asked to do. It drives ADs crazy. Not that you have to be in a full speed run—but extremely close. ADs like their teams to be quick and to think on their feet.

DON'T PANIC!

On the set everyone will have questions for you. Everybody thinks that their question is the most important and should be answered first. You will learn as you go along—

what is a little spark of concern and what is a Code Red. It's not constructive to panic. Stay calm and everyone around you will stay calm (in the ideal world). Tell yourself, "It is only a movie. I am not performing a heart transplant; I am not teaching third world countries to speak English; I am not fighting a raging forest fire. I am making a movie." It is a piece of celluloid that will make people laugh and cry. Whatever the problem, there is a solution. It might take a few minutes to find it.

In the meantime, do not panic. Count to Ten.

DON'T BE AFRAID TO ADMIT YOU DON'T KNOW SOMETHING

It's not a big deal if you do not know. Everyone has been where you are and it is okay not to know. Raise your hand and admit it.

DON'T BE AFRAID TO ADMIT WHEN YOU ARE WRONG OR HAVE MADE A MISTAKE

Everyone makes mistakes. It is a relief to admit that you have made a mistake. I repeat: Everyone makes mistakes. Admit it. You will sleep better.

DON'T BE AFRAID; IT'S ONLY A MOVIE!

By entering film production you have taken a giant leap of faith. It's not an easy career to choose. The hours are long and the work can be thankless. However, once you have committed, work from your passion and keep your eyes on your goal. It will be tough at first to swallow your pride and ride the learning curve. Hollywood has many incredibly talented, creative, insecure, petrified people—

just like you. Keep swimming and eventually you will get to where you want to go. Follow your gut instincts and show no fear.

HAVE FUN!

In the beginning you may doubt why you ever became involved in this crazy business. The work can be grueling at times. However, once you get a sense of how the set operates, how you fit in and how to do your work proficiently, you will start enjoying yourself. It's not brain surgery. If you are not having fun though, stop right now!

[Note: Part II covers the logistics of the set: base camp, the layout of the set, and heating and air conditioning. In the event you are thrown head first into a job, this is a rough guideline on how to get around. If you need to learn more about the nitty gritty of lock ups, radios and extras, jump ahead to Chapter Six.]

"You have never been inside a film studio before?"

"Only once. Years ago."

"It will interest you, as a phenomenon. You see, the film studio of today is the palace of the sixteenth century. There one sees what Shakespeare saw: the absolute power of the tyrant, the courtiers, the flatterers, the jesters, the cunningly ambitious intriguers. There are fantastically beautiful women, there are incompetent favorites. There are great men who are suddenly disgraced. There is a most insane extravagance, and unexpected parsimony over a few pence. There is enormous splendor, which is a sham; and also horrible squalor hidden behind the scenery. There are vast schemes, abandoned because of some caprice. There are secrets which everybody knows and no one speaks of. There are even one or two honest advisers. These are the court fools, who speak the deepest wisdom in puns, lest they should be taken seriously. They grimace and tear their hair privately and weep."

Christopher Isherwood
Prater Violet (1945)

Part II

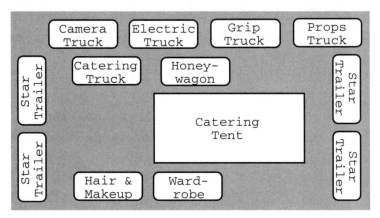

Base Camp

3

Base Camp

LOGISTICS

Each day you arrive on the set there is a basic layout to the operations. Here is a breakdown starting with the trucks in base camp and working toward the set. The newer you are, the farther away from the camera you will be. Moving closer to the heart of the filmmaking process is a right that is earned over time. Do not be discouraged. Keep plugging along and one day you will be standing right next to the director of photography as he pulls out his hair and gazes at the giant 200K in the sky.

THE HONEYWAGON

This vehicle is a long trailer with a few rooms *(bangers)* and a couple of bathrooms. Some actors are contractually guaranteed a two-banger (the doors slide open between them). The 2nd AD will have a good idea who gets what. In the morning, one of your jobs may be to label the doors to the rooms. All you will need is some white tape and a black marking pen. You can write the character's name on their respective doors. (I always use the character's name for security reasons.)

Luckily this is where the bathrooms are. At times when it is busy, the Loo or 10-100 is your only warm, safe place from people who need you. [A tip: If you are calling your

1st or 2nd AD and they are not answering and you do not see them near the set, they are probably one of two places—detained in the producer's trailer getting reprimanded or 10-100]. Do not keep calling them, unless of course someone is seriously injured. They will turn up.

If you are at a location without bathrooms, make sure the honeywagon stays until the entire crew has wrapped. The hard-working electricians who are still wrapping out cable three hours after everyone else has left should not be left without a working bathroom or two.

STAR WAGONS

The big stars get their own trailers. Most productions use separate trailers rather than recreational vehicles (RVs) as trailers do not require additional drivers. Depending on their deals, the producer and director have decent sized trailers as well.

HAIR & MAKEUP TRAILER

This is where the powdering and puffing occur. Here are a few tips for this highly sensitive trailer:
- Always knock.
- Announce that you are "stepping up" (entering) or "stepping down" (exiting). Someone may be applying a tattoo or eye makeup or doing very precise work and you do not want to startle them.
- Limit the food in the trailer. If the actor forgot to eat, it's a fine line. How can a makeup artist get anything done while an actor is eating?

WARDROBE TRAILER

Wardrobe people are some of the most inventive people I know. I have seen them make something out of nothing. They have all these little doo-dads that hold things together. This is where they keep all their clothes and accessories. This is also where the extras will line up to get their clothes.

CAMERA AND SOUND TRUCK

The camera truck is always the truck closest to the set since the camera gear is valuable and most essential. You will become familiar with the camera truck because if the sound guys are on there, then so are the radios. It is also the only truck with the power left on when everyone leaves. The film and cameras are highly sensitive so a great deal of care goes into the truck.

Remember that camera people are some of the most meticulous people you will ever meet, especially the loader and the 2nd assistant. These guys can be fired over things that may seem inconsequential but when projected on a screen at dailies, suddenly seem monumental. A hair in the gate of the camera or dust in the lens can completely ruin a day's work. They have a great deal of responsibility and sometimes they project their tension. Smile and nod. If you are on their truck, respect their rules and work with them.

The camera truck usually has two entrances: one on the side and one in the back (where the tailgate comes down). Usually the radios are in the back near the tailgate and all the important camera stuff is toward the front. If you are in charge of the radios, (see Chapter 16 on Radios) work out your system and determine how you will distribute and account for them every day.

In the camera truck toward the front will be a door that looks as if it could maybe be a bathroom. *Do not open it.* This is a *changing room* for the film. It is a darkroom, and nine times out of ten there is a loader in there feverishly trying to thread the film through the magazine correctly.

PROP TRUCK

The extras will go to the prop truck usually to receive their props. For this reason, it's good to know its location. By your second or third show, you will be able to identify each truck from its exterior, or by glimpsing what equipment is hanging on the walls

SPECIAL EFFECTS (FX) TRUCK

Most FX trucks are like little chemistry labs. There always seems to be someone in there fiddling with something dangerous. If you go in there, make sure your hair is tucked in your hat and you keep your arms and legs close to your body. You never know. This is also where the heaters are. Good to know for those thirty-below-zero night shoots.

GRIP TRUCK

This is where all the grip equipment is stored. If you need rope or tape or sand bags, this is the place.

ELECTRIC TRUCK

Lighting equipment, stands, flags and gels are stored on the electric truck (spark) truck.

FUEL TRUCK

A truck with fuel so the company always has fuel for the vehicles.

WATER TRUCK

The truck used to wet down streets if it is called for in the script. This truck can also be used when rain effects are needed. They can wet down dusty roads so people do not kick up as much dust around the set.

CATERING TRUCK

This is where all the main meals are prepared.

CRAFT SERVICE TRUCK

Also near the set. Where all the major snacks are kept and where most significant snacking occurs.

LAYOUT

The trucks are near enough to the set that it is not a huge hike but far enough away so that we do not hear the generator or see the catering truck in the shot. As the setups change and coverage is shot, certain things may need to be moved out of the shot. Usually the ADs will let you know so you can start getting things moved early.

"When I first moved to LA, I was so broke that I slept on someone's couch and had only enough money to buy a chocolate bar and a cup of coffee every day. I was working for free as a set PA, trying to land my first real PA gig. I have not stopped working since then—only now I get paid."

Jeffrey Wetzel, 1st Assistant Director
Replacement Killers, Last Man Standing, Tremors II, Mr. Holland's Opus

4

The Set

Each set has several common denominators. When you arrive at a new location—check out where the following things are:

THE PHONE

Every set will have at least one phone, be it a mobile phone or a land line. Sometimes you will have to use a pay phone, so make sure to have lots of quarters on hand. If you are the keeper of the set phone, encourage whoever is using it to return it to you before they pass it on to someone else. It is impossible to find if they hand it over to somebody else. Make sure it is turned off when you return it to your holster. If there is a hard line, turn the ringer off and learn the phone number in case the office needs to call.

KNOW THY COPIER

Know it. Love it. Learn to use it. Master the copier and you will have people eating out of your hand. Hopefully you will have a copier in the production trailer. Make sure it always has paper (lots of legal size—for making 100 or more call sheets), learn how to un-jam it, and where to put the toner. If you do not have a copier and need to use the one in the Production office, be ready. Know it. Love it. Learn it. Remember, the production office is your best friend. Sometimes they will run off the call sheets for you.

Other times they will be so swamped that you will need to run them off yourself. If the copier gets jammed—try to fix it yourself. Most of the newer machines have digital displays to tell you what is wrong. Follow the blinking arrows. The new ones do everything but make coffee.

Here is a quick list of tips on your new friend the copy machine:

1. Feed it paper—the size and color you want.
2. Keep the numbers low. Try not to make more than 25 to 30 copies at a time.
3. Keep an eye on it while it is doing its thing.
4. Try to un-jam it yourself.
5. Take out your colored paper when you are finished!
6. Hit clear all when you are done—for the next person who uses it.
7. Count to ten if there is a problem. Assess it.
8. Do not be afraid of things like toner and dry ink. Roll up your sleeves and get dirty!
9. Clean off the copier with window cleaner before you begin.
10. Know it. Love it. Learn it.

BATHROOMS

Know where they are—know how to get to them. Make some signs if the bathrooms are in out of the way locations.

GREEN ROOM

This is where the actors hang out if base camp is far away from where you are shooting. It's a place they can hang out in between shots.

CRAFT SERVICE

This is the place where the calories are found.

EXTRAS HOLDING

This is where the extras hang out when they are not needed on the set.

"When I first moved to LA, I looked in the production guide in *The Hollywood Reporter*. The next day I dropped off 60 resumes around town. I got two blisters and a job."

Derek Vermaas, Production Secretary
Dante's Peak, If These Walls Could Talk,
Mi Familia, Nowhere, The Doom Generation

5

Heating &
Air Conditioning

Every indoor set has one of two problems. It's either too hot or too cold. For this reason the production department is in charge of keeping the temperature at a comfortable level.

ON AND OFF

As the crew gets closer to rolling camera, a PA is usually put in charge of starting or stopping the air conditioning (or heat). If this is your job, make sure you listen closely to the radio. Air conditioners and heaters make too much noise to be kept running during a take. If the air conditioning unit is large it will be placed outside, away from the set. You will have to listen closely to your radio because the air conditioning or heating unit is loud and there may be other outside noises around you. It has become the production department's job to keep people warm or cool. You will find yourself learning how to turn on the propane heaters (be careful) or bringing a fan in for an actor who is sweating profusely in between takes. Hey, it's a glamorous job, I know! If you hear that the camera has started rolling and you have not turned your air conditioner off, it's a good idea to turn it off in case. Better to be scolded afterwards than to have ruined the sound on the entire take.

SAFETY

As I mentioned before, *be careful and be safe*. The special effects (FX) team is in charge of lighting the propane heaters. Sometimes they are too busy and you may find yourself having to do the job. Make sure you check the gas and lighter switch before you begin. Once the heater is lit, do not let people stand too close. (I cannot tell you how many beautiful jackets I have seen with big burn marks on them.) If you smell something burning, check your gloves. They might be melting; or, the heater may be leaking. Turn it off and tell someone from FX.

STINGERS

To power up (juice) anything on the set you will need a plug with power. Never assume on a set that you can plug in anywhere. *Always* check with the Electric department. Explain to them what you are trying to do. They will help you unless they are very busy at the time. They will probably give you a *stinger,* or extension cord, that can plug into a usable outlet.

SOUND

Air conditioning units, fans, vents and heaters are probably the worst causes of unnecessary noise while shooting. Toilets flushing, vents releasing air, traffic and music can cause sound problems as well.

Part III

"What are the shots for today? It's simple. It's bada-boom bada-boom and then after lunch, we do the reverse of bada-boom bada-boom. Then we punch in tighter and do bing bing."

Deirdre Horgan, Script Supervisor
The Preacher's Wife, Nixon,
Natural Born Killers, Heaven & Earth

6

A Day in the Life of a set PA

DAY TO DAY

There is no typical day in the life of a set PA. This is what makes the job so interesting. PAs do a myriad of tasks from day to day. Every film is different and the operations and procedures will vary from film to film. Duties of a PA on a nonunion film are quite different from PA duties on a union film. There is a routine flow through the day. I have listed the elements in their daily priority order. Your day is divided into five parts:

- Crew Call
- Setting Up the Shot and Shooting
- Lunch
- Setting Up the Shot and Shooting
- Wrap

This chapter deals with *crew call, lunch* and *wrap*. In following chapters, I will discuss what occurs during *setting up the shot* and *shooting* parts of the day. Other specific jobs surface throughout the day and I will discuss those as well.

Crew Call

This section will give you an idea of how each morning begins.

A GOOD HABIT

Every night after work (or early in the morning), take out your *call sheet.* Look at the scenes you will be shooting the following day. Open your script and read the scenes scheduled for that day. Note which actors will work and what the day's work involves. This preparation will give you a good head start.

BREAKFAST

When the crew arrives, the first thing they will do is eat breakfast. Try to get to the set a little early so you can eat. Once everyone arrives, you will not have much time. Make a mental note of who is arriving. When actors and *stand-ins* start to arrive you should let the 1st and 2nd AD know on the radio so they can decide who is *going into the works.* Let the 1st AD know when the director and DP have arrived as well. Check with them and see if they would like some breakfast brought to them. Sometimes they will eat with the crew. One PA usually hangs out by the catering truck to take breakfast orders for the people who do not have time to eat. They also keep track of those people still eating in the tent or eating area. As you take a breakfast order, write it down and hand it into the chef. When you deliver breakfast, make sure you have utensils, napkins, drinks, etc. Most of the breakfast orders will be for the actors, hair, makeup and wardrobe.

CHECKING OUT RADIOS

As everyone arrives, one PA will be handing out *radios or walkie-talkies.* Make sure the 1st and 2nd ADs have their radios with fresh batteries first thing.

CHECKING IN THE EXTRAS OR BACKGROUND

One or two PAs will be *wrangling the extras* as they arrive for work. The extras need to eat breakfast and then they, too, need to get ready for filming.

SIDES

Sides are pages of the script usually containing the scenes to be completed for the day. It has become popular to reduce these sides and staple them to the day's call sheet. Each page is about $5^1/_2$" x $8^1/_2$" when reduced. When the key department heads (*keys*) arrive, make sure they have their sides. If for some reason there are no sides, you will probably be asked to make them. To do this you will need your current script, scissors, stapler and a copy machine. Look at the call sheet and note the scenes to be shot for the day. Go to the scenes in your script and pull them. Reduce a call sheet for the first page and then reduce the scene to be shot. Cut them down to size and staple them. On some shows, the script changes constantly. It is important to keep your script up to date for this reason. If you make sides with a page that has been revised, and the actor has not received the revision, the actor might become upset. Keep it current.

REHEARSAL

First up after breakfast is rehearsal. Most of the actors will have just arrived. The director will block the scene and work out the camera moves. Then the actors will go back to get ready and the crew will light the scene using stand-ins in place of the actors. Make sure the stand-ins and key department heads know when a rehearsal is taking place. This way they can be present to see how the scene will go and dictate to their departments accordingly.

SAFETY MEETING

As the cast and crew gather for the first shot, the 1st AD will review the shooting day and any safety hazards. The meeting is then noted on the production report.

Lunch Activities

WATCHING THE LINE

When lunch is called, one PA usually counts the number of people who go through the line. Watch out for people who are not involved in your production. They may try to sneak into line to get a free lunch. This has to be handled very diplomatically. If you are working in a shady area of town, there will probably be a security guard or two who can help you with this. If you are counting you may find it helpful to use "counter" and click it as each person goes through the line. The production is generally charged for lunch by the quantity of plates that are served. Part of being involved in the AD department is helping the studio keep track of costs by observing when people come in and out of work and lunch.

If you are watching the line, once the last crew member has gone through, you will inform the 1st AD. She will then say, "Okay, we are back in 1/2 hour." It is industry practice that a one-half hour lunch is taken from the time the last person has gone through the line. If you are working on the lot (at one of the studios) lunch may be one hour. In this case, lunch is up to you, as long as you are back in one hour. {Note: On union shoots, lunch is six hours after crew call.}

There is a pecking order in the lunch line. Certain people are allowed to take cuts (or jump ahead of everyone else). Actors, the director and other parties who need to get back to work soon or may need to attend *dailies* usually eat first. There may be a separate line for the extras that you will also need to watch. If they share the line with the crew, you need to make sure that the crew eats first and then the extras. If there are many extras you might help hand out the box lunches.

LUNCH COUNT

The caterer will give the AD department a lunch count before they leave that day. This is a form that goes with the day's paperwork. Your count and the caterer's count should be exact, or vary by one or two. The caterers arrive at their number by determining how many plates were served. This number is reflected on the production report for the studio.

FRESH BATTERIES

It's a good idea to hand out fresh batteries at lunch, particularly to the ADs.

YOUR TEAM

Many times the 1st and 2nd AD will go off to discuss the
call sheet for the next day over lunch and often forget to
eat. It's your job to look out for your team. Ask them on
the radio if they would like some lunch. Make sure you
have the menu handy because they will ask you what the
caterer is serving. As you get to know your ADs, you will
find out all of their little idiosyncratic eating habits. Make
a mental note of these. It will save you time down the road.
Sometimes they will want something not on the menu. Go
to the caterer and let them know. They will always help
you.

WHEN ARE WE BACK?

This is the most common question asked at lunch time,
that and, "What is for dessert?" It has become industry
practice that we are back one half hour after the last person went through the line. Keep track of it. If the AD asks
you at 1:30 P.M., "When are we back?", what will you say?
The last person went through at 1:20 P.M. so you can pre-
sume that we are back at 1:50 P.M. Now you can phrase
that two ways. "We are back at 1:50 P.M. or we are back in
20 minutes." I tend to think the "We are back in 20 minutes" version works better. If you say we are back at 1:50
P.M. and someone's watch is five minutes fast there will be
some confusion. For this reason, I would say, "We are back
in 20 minutes." No confusion. When we are back, it's your
job to let everyone know. Usually the PAs split up the duty.
Someone shouts, "We're back!", in the catering tent, someone announces it over the radio on ALL channels, someone at base camp, "We're back!", someone near the trucks,

and someone near the set. This way everyone knows that lunch is over and it's time to go back to work.

FRENCH HOURS

If a show is on a tight schedule, sometimes the crew takes a vote and if the majority is in favor, they waive their meal breaks. The crew works through the day and catering brings around trays of finger foods.

Wrap

When the company wraps, the AD department kicks into action. If you blink you will miss half of it.

CALL SHEETS

The call sheet is a plan for the next day's work. It tells when we will start, what we want to achieve, who needs to be present, where we will be located and many other specifics. When we wrap, everyone needs to know what time they should to be back at work. Usually after lunch, the call sheet is approved and sent to the office to be photocopied. If there is a copier in the production trailer, you will probably be copying the call sheets. The 100 or so copies of the call sheets should be back and ready to be handed out at wrap.

TURNAROUND

Turnaround is the rest time that has been contractually agreed for you to have before returning to work the next day (or night). Unfortunately, not everyone takes the same call time or has the same turnaround. Depending on an individual's contract and their particular union's rules, some people have different turnaround times. Many actors have a 12 hour turnaround. Most of the time the crew has a 10 hour turnaround. The rules vary depending on a few variables. Is the show union or nonunion? Are you on location? Is it an East Coast show?

FORCED CALL

If the production decides to bring people back before their required turnaround, this is called a *forced call.* Forced calls must be approved by the unit production manager and producer since they involve financial penalties. Forced calls for actors and crew differ. If an actor finishes shooting at 10 P.M. one night and is due on the set the next morning at 6:00 A.M., there will be a financial penalty for breaking the actor's turnaround and forcing his call. It depends on your contract with the production. For this reason when you wrap, producers and ADs will decide what time the company can bring everyone back to work the next day.

FLYING THE CALL SHEETS

Nearing wrap time, if you are handed a fat envelope, look at it. If it contains the call sheets, let the 2nd AD know. He or she will probably want to see them. Show the 1st AD who will usually ask you to hang onto them. DO NOT PUT THEM DOWN. Everyone is going to want a call sheet before wrap. This is dangerous. If you give someone a call sheet early and some information on the call sheet changes . . . guess whose fault it is if that person does not show up on time because he did not get the changed information? Yours. For this reason hold onto the call sheets until you are told to *fly them (distribute them).* If someone says they are leaving and needs a call sheet, let the 2nd AD decide whether or not to give it out.

If the call times change then you will probably get the task of changing the time on them. The call time will usually be *pushed*. This means the call time is advanced a certain amount of time to meet turnaround times. This would be for *general crew call*. This means that actors and the vanity team (hair, makeup and wardrobe) will also adjust their calls accordingly. It is the production department's job to make sure that everyone has a call time and knows when to report to work the next day. When you hand out the call sheets, make sure you verbalize it, too. "General crew call is 7:00 A.M." or "Calls are pushed one hour. Call is at 8:00 A.M." If *calls stand*, it means the producers want to stick to the call time on the call sheet. At the end of the night the 2nd AD will go through the call sheet and ask everyone who told them their call time. Check off on a call sheet when you give a crew member their call sheet. It's easy to forget. If you are on location, it may be your job to deliver the call sheets to the hotel and slide them under everyone's door. Make sure you have a call sheet. You may be busy taking care of everyone else, but it is your responsibility to ask for your call time. Once you have handed out all the call sheets it's time to take care of *out times.*

An out time is the time reflected on your time card as the time you completed work for the day or are officially off the clock. Out times indicate how people are paid, and help keep an accurate record for the producers and the studio. As people are leaving, a PA usually stands at a general exit to get out times. Sometimes people need to add their travel time or they ask you to add it. Make sure you know what the travel time is to and from location. It is usually somewhere on the call sheet. Again, use your call sheet as a worksheet and write the crew members out time next to their name. Write down what people tell you are their out times. It is up to the 2nd AD and production manager to decide if they are taking too long to finish for the day.

Out times will be verbalized to you in two ways. Each show is different. One way is the actual time. "I am out at 7:30 P.M. or 19:30 hours." Or, they will say, "I am out at 19.5." It depends on the studio. "Nineteen point five" also means 7:30 P.M. Nineteen (or nineteen hundred hours) is the equivalent in military time for 7:00 P.M. and .5 is calculated using the following equation. There are ten six-minute increments in an hour. Round to the closest six-minute increment and you will have your official out time.

.1 = 06 minutes past the hour (6 x 1)
.2 = 12 minutes past the hour (6 x 2)
.3 = 18 minutes past the hour (6 x 3)
.4 = 24 minutes past the hour (6 x 4)
.5 = 30 minutes past the hour (6 x 5)
.6 = 36 minutes past the hour (6 x 6)
.7 = 42 minutes past the hour (6 x 7)
.8 = 48 minutes past the hour (6 x 8)
.9 = 54 minutes past the hour (6 x 9)
.0 = 0   minutes past the hour (6 x 10, or 0)

Whatever their out time is will help you to determine their turnaround. This is why it is so important to get the actors on their way as soon as you wrap.

LOADING OUT THE VANS

Usually most people will catch a van to and from location. If this is the case, one van will usually leave right at wrap with actors and anyone else who is able to leave right away. The next van will start to fill up. While people are in the van it is a good time to give them their call sheets and check their out times. Give a verbal holler if the van is leaving shortly. The crew can hurry and get their stuff together and get out of there. If an actor is stuck in a crew van, try to get the van on its way immediately so that you do not run into a turnaround problem.

LAST PERSON OUT

It is the AD department's job to wait for the last person to finish work. It is usually the electricians who take a while to tear down and put their equipment away. Noting who is the last person and at what time he finished is required on the production report to keep the studio informed. It is important that the medic stays as well, in case there is an accident while the grips and electricians are striking (tearing down) the set.

CHECKING IN RADIOS

While everyone is wrapping, make sure you collect their radios. If you have them labeled by department, this will help you a great deal as far as checking them off your checklist. Make sure you get the batteries charging as well. If you are missing a radio, let the 2nd AD know so it can be reflected on the production report.

"I heard a story about a young woman who got her break as a PA and wanted to do a good job. The company was shooting in a very shady area of Los Angeles and they sent this girl to a lock up on an isolated street where a few drunk bums were sleeping on the curbs. After they started rolling, a drunk bum came up to her and started talking to her slurring and slobbering. She was petrified but kept quiet. The bum then vomited all over her shoes. The girl stood there, quiet, keeping things locked down and under control. She did not even scream. When they yelled, "Cut" . . . she screamed and help was on the way. That's true dedication."

April

7

Lock Ups

WHAT IS A LOCK UP?

A *lock up* is a method of controlling unwanted or extraneous noise and activity immediately before and during the
filming of a shot. A movie set is a controlled environment.
Things need to be quiet and the shot clear for shooting. In
order to accomplish this, the ADs use lock ups. In a lock
up it is your job to keep everyone who not designated to
be in the shot quiet, and out of the shot. Usually the 2nd
AD will set the lock ups (or tell you what your area of
responsibility is) so the 1st AD can attend to the director
and everyone's questions. The 2nd AD will get the *frame-
lines* (the area of the shot that the camera is seeing) from
the 1st AD so he or she knows what the shot is. Once they
determine what the shot is, they set the lock ups.

HANDLING YOUR LOCK UP

The key to taking care of your area of concern is to not
look at the action. Look everywhere *but* the camera.
Anticipate where your *bogies* (people, animals, cars or
unidentified flying objects that are not part of the shot)
might appear. Everyone from the AD department will be
spread out on the bigger shots. Locking up a public place
can be particularly difficult, especially if you do not have
many PAs. Usually the 2nd is just off the set—near the 1st

AD. One PA is deep camera left (out of frame) and another camera right. Craft service and extras holding tend to be noisy places, so sometimes someone will also be stationed there.

YOUR LOCK UP

The farther away your lock up is from the action, the newer you are. The more experienced you get, the closer you get to the camera. Your first lock up will probably be on some abandoned highway with no one around as far as the eye can see. You will think to yourself, what am I doing here? This is not filmmaking . . . this is horrible! Then the camera car speeds by with the entire crew strapped on, cameras rolling, shooting a high speed chase scene. The dust kicks up around you and you know why you are there. You made sure that no one crossed in front of the speeding car, enabling the crew to shoot the scene.

LOCKING UP A STREET

If you are on the street, you need to exercise some caution. Sometimes you will be asked to hold the pedestrian traffic. People are very curious about movie-making. They will want to see what is going on. If you are not shooting, simply invite them to keep on walking past the set. Explain to the passerby that it is a very hectic day and the company is very busy. Always try to be as polite as possible. People can get very irate when they are in a hurry and have an unexpected delay. Use your "pleases" and "thank-yous" and *never touch them.* It will be your instinct to grab them as they almost walk into an important scene. Do not. This person has no idea what is happening. Grabbing them may cause a bigger disturbance. "Pssst" seems to work or "Hey" or "Yoo Hoo" or waving your arms. Do your best and stay alert. If you are alert and keep looking around, you should be able to intercept any bogies.

HOLDING TRAFFIC

When locking up an area, you may need to hold traffic. This means that you will try to prevent pedestrians or cars or both from passing through the shot. Try to put your body in between the people or cars that may ruin the shot. Be safe! Exercise caution and do not step in front of a moving car. Often you may have to hold the pedestrians or traffic for a long time. You may be far away from the primary area of action or at a remote lock up. The people being held will start to get restless. If you are at some remote lock up (which is where they stick the new PAs) and are not sure if the company is rolling, do not try the radio! If cameras are rolling, it's not a good idea. Hold the traffic and try to see what action is happening around the camera. If you cannot see the camera, then listen to your radio. If people are talking, chances are cameras are not rolling.

Once the camera cuts, the AD will announce, "Release traffic." At that point, you can let the cars and pedestrians go on their way. Sometimes pedestrians or the people in their cars get very angry when they have to wait. Be polite and smile. As you hold people, they may ask what film you are shooting. It's good to have a little one-liner about the film (for example: It's a monster coming-of-age film about a giant deadly slime creature that is sent to earth to destroy humanity. The monster ends up having a change of heart when he saves a boy from drowning in Niagara Falls.) Your main focus should always be on your lock up.

BELLS AND WHISTLES

When you are shooting on a stage, lock ups are a bit easier. It is a much more controlled environment. You may be assigned to ring "the bell" when the camera is rolling and when we've cut.

One Long Ring: ROLLING

Two Short Rings: CUT

With bell duty comes light duty. A revolving siren-type light outside the stage lets people know when cameras are rolling. The switches are usually together. Be sure to test the bell before you start shooting.

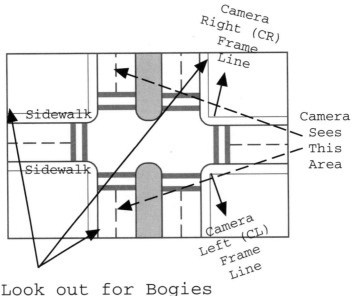

Look out for Bogies

Lock up diagram

8

The Shot

Each shot in a film is carefully planned, rehearsed and set up with specific intentions in mind. Before filming a scene the following routine usually takes place:

TALKING ABOUT THE SHOT

Before each shot is setup the key department heads get together and discuss it. Usually the director, 1st AD, director of photography and gaffer will walk off and huddle together in conversation. There is much nodding and pointing. Then like football, they break away and everyone gets busy again. The director may talk to the actors in base camp or scribble notes on his script. The DP convenes with the gaffer. They then put their troops to work. The AD communicates with everyone else. The actors are called to the set.

REHEARSAL WITH THE ACTORS

When the actors come to the set, they will be in some stage of going through the works, or they may have just arrived. As the set PA, always keep an eye on the actors. They might wander to craft service or outside for some fresh air. The next thing you know there is an APB (All Points Bulletin) out on them.

Sometimes there is a protocol for calling the actors to

the set. If you have two big *leads* (actors) sometimes one will not go to set until the other is already there. It's a power thing. Do your best to get everyone to the set. Usually the 1st AD will announce "Rehearsal with actors only" or "Closed rehearsal." This means the director and the actors (and occasionally the script supervisor or the 1st AD). You may need extra sides standing by as the directors and actors will be *blocking the scene*.

During the closed rehearsal, the crew will hang out at craft service or around the set and will proceed to ask you a million times "Is it still closed? Can we watch yet?" Their intentions are good—they want to know how their department is involved in the scene. Each department will, at some point in the movie, have a distorted perspective of the film. This movie is about props. No, wait. It's a movie about beavers. It's a movie about special effects makeup. No, it's not. No, no. It's about a generator that is sabotaged. No, you've gotten it all wrong. It's about angora sweaters! It's a condition that happens on every film. All of a sudden each department thinks it's a movie about their department. Each department wants to be prepared, to make sure everything is perfect. Smile and nod and communicate. Remember you are wearing a headset. You are a pipeline to the set and, in a small way, you can help.

TECHNICAL REHEARSAL

All departments watch the rehearsal with the actors. Make sure that the stand-ins are at the rehearsal. They need to watch the action carefully as the actors are about to go back into the works and they will have to re-enact the blocking. If it is a complicated scene the actors may go through it several times to sort out any glitches in the scene. After the *technical rehearsal*, actors go back to hair and makeup to finish preparations. The other crew goes into a *"lighting mode."*

THE LIGHTING MODE

The stand-ins take their places; the crew lights the scene; and the camera sets up for the shot. Dolly tracks are laid down; lights are moved and adjusted. Camera changes a lens and sets focus marks; they work out the dolly move. It's a busy time for the crew. Stay out of the way and keep an eye out for anyone who needs help. It's a good time to see if anyone needs water or coffee.

SECOND TEAM

During lighting mode is when second team works. They have to stand and move as the actors will when the scene is shot. Keep them close. If it looks as if you are about to go into a *new deal* (new set up), start getting your second team ready. You are going to hear about it if they are not there when the 1st AD needs them. Good stand-ins are always there and you never have to ask twice. Some, however, disappear and wander away. Keep them close.

ACTORS READY

Once the actors are ready, they can relax until the camera is ready. It's about 50-50 who is done first—the actors or the camera. If camera is ready then the actors will head to the set.

CAMERA READY

If camera is done first, then the crew hangs out until the actors are ready. Like everything else, each show is different. If special effects makeup is needed, the actors may take longer getting ready. At the same time, if it is a difficult camera setup with intricate lighting, camera may take a little longer.

REHEARSAL WITH FIRST TEAM AND BACKGROUND

Once the camera is ready, you may do some run-throughs with background so that everything is ready to rock. Once the first team (the actors) arrive on set, you may do a rehearsal with first team, sometimes with background and sometimes not. This is a good time to check your lock up and see if everything is going to flow smoothly from your area of responsibility.

LOCKING IT UP

Once everyone is in place, the set needs to be quiet. The 2nd AD will set the lock ups and place PAs in the right areas. Their aim is twofold: maintaining absolute quiet on the set; and keeping unwanted people and things off the set. Once you have your lock up, assess your area. Are you cueing background? Do they know what their action is? Where could your bogies come from? What is the scene? Will you be given delayed cues from the 1st AD? Is there equipment running in your area that needs to be turned off when you shoot? Do you need to cue an actor also? Anticipate. Anticipate.

FINAL TOUCHES

Once the area is controlled, the 1st AD will call for final touches. This gives hair, makeup and wardrobe their last chance to spritz, smooth, powder, puff, fluff and fold anything on the actors.

LET'S SHOOT

Once everything is ready, it's time to shoot. The 1st AD will call the shots:

```
                    1ST AD
                (Over walkie-talkie)
            Nice and quiet please.

                    2ND AD
                (Over walkie-talkie)
            Quiet please

                    SET PA
                (Projecting loudly)
            Quiet please.

                    1ST AD
            Stand by. Here we go.

                    2ND AD
            Stand by.

                    SET PA
            Stand by!

                    1ST AD
            And.... roll please
The camera turns over.

                    2ND AD
            Rolling!

                    SET PA
            ROLLING!
The set is absolutely quiet.
```

       SOUND
   This is OUT COLD, SCENE 101,
   TAKE 1
   SPEED! (or SOUND SPEED)

       CAMERA
   SPEED.

The 2nd Assistant camera claps the slate.

       CAMERA
   Marker.

      1ST AD
   BACKGROUND ACTION!!

      2ND AD
   BACKGROUND!

The background starts to move.

      DIRECTOR
   ACTION!

      1ST AD
    (Sotto into radio)
   Action. Action.

Allison stands in the middle of the bank in her
pajamas holding the teller at gun point. All of a
sudden a police car engulfed in flames crashes
through the door. People scatter in every direction.

      DIRECTOR
   CUT!! That was great!

      1ST AD
   That's a cut.

      2ND AD
   We've cut.

      SET PA
   CUT! We've cut!

Everyone stops moving. The fire in the car is
extinguished. The area is made safe for another
take. The director and DP look at the playback.
The director converses with the actors, finessing
the scene.

```
                    1ST AD
         Going again. Back to one every-
         body.

                    SET PA
         Going again! Back to one,
         please.
```

Actors and background shuffle to their starting
positions (number one).

```
                    1ST AD
           Here we go. Lock it up.

                    SET PA
           Stand by, please.
```

That's pretty much the *ideal world*. A million things will affect how smoothly all of this flows. For the most part, this is how it happens. You will always project the loudest for *"rolling."* However, it is as important to let people know when we have *"cut"* so they can move again. Loud projections are generally unnecessary in most other situations.

Once the scene is complete and the coverage for that scene has been obtained the camera will change direction and the company will go into a *new deal*. The crew will begin again with talking about the shot.

```
                    1ST AD
         New Deal. We're going roundy
         round.

                    SET PA
         NEW DEAL!!
```

"The film business
is a shallow money
trench. A long,
plastic hallway
where thieves and
pimps run free and
good men die like
dogs."

Hunter S. Thompson

9

Paperwork

No task is complete without paperwork, and the movie business is no exception. It's called show *business* for a reason. Try to think of your job from the studio's point of view. Every good business always backs up its work with some type of tangible documentation. Doing paperwork is a necessary evil and, once you understand that, things will not seem so overwhelming.

Daily Paperwork

There are certain forms of paperwork that will roll across your desk, or rather your clipboard, every day. At the end of every day's (or night's) shooting, gather all the necessary documentation and ship it to the production office in a large envelope—the pouch. Following is a list of those documents.

THE CALL SHEET

This very valuable tool tells you everything you need to know about work that is scheduled to be completed that day. There is also some information about future shooting days. The 2nd AD usually prepares the call sheet. [Note: If you have the opportunity, ask the 2nd AD to give you a copy on a disk (or practice writing it out in longhand) so you can try preparing a call sheet at home. Preparing a call sheet shows you exactly how much work it takes to pull together one day of shooting. As you practice, a million questions will come to your mind. How long does it take to get Shirley Templeton ready in the morning? How many extras will you need? How long will it take to light the first scene? Are maps attached to the new location? Do the prop people need to provide anything special? Will there be a *wetdown*? How many horses will you need? Are there campfires in this scene? Usually, many of these specific questions can be answered by referring to the *shooting schedule.]*

THE PRODUCTION REPORT

The production report is a record of what actually happened during the shooting day (the call sheet lists what one hopes to accomplish). It is a legal document used by the studio to account for each activity throughout the day, and, therefore it is very important that you maintain an accurate account for each item. If you look carefully at the example on pg. 178, you will see how each department is accounted for. On nonunion shows, if you get the opportunity to prepare the production report, do it! It will give you an in-depth idea of how each department fits into the report and accounts to the studio.

TIME CARDS

Each crew member fills out a time card each week to be paid. Usually it is the AD department's job to hand out time cards on the day they are due. Make sure you call the accounting department to order some more if you find you are running low. Union members have different color time cards from nonunion members. Often the 1st and 2nd ADs are too busy to fill out their time cards and will ask you do it for them. Make sure you get their times from the production report so they are paid the appropriate over-time. Some crew members are paid for travel time to and from their homes (or hotel). The travel time to location is noted every day on the call sheet. During the day, or at wrap, collect the time cards. Prepare an envelope in the production trailer that says:

Production Name

Time Cards

Date

If you want to get a jump on things, make up enough of these envelopes for the whole show in advance. Then you will not find yourself scrambling at wrap time looking for an empty envelope—it will be all ready for you.

SAG SHEET

Actors are paid from the SAG Sheet. The SAG sheet (see pg. 180) records the time each actor arrives, eats lunch, and departs and arrives back home (or hotel, if appli-cable). When the actors wrap, they sign out on the SAG sheet. The producers review the actors' hours, and then send (or fax) a report to the studio and to SAG.

VOUCHERS

In order for your extras to be paid, they will need to fill out a multipart voucher. The extra keeps the pink copy. The white and yellow copies go to accounting. If you are the PA assigned to the extras, you and the extras coordinator will compile all the vouchers at wrap. You will then tally who left when and mark this on the bottom of the production report. The stand-ins are either paid by voucher or with a time card.

CAMERA AND SOUND REPORTS

The camera report records how much film was used for the day and how much was wasted. It also tallies the amount of remaining film stock and any incoming film stock received that day. The sound report records how many quarter-inch reels or DAT tape were used for that day of filming.

SCRIPT SUPERVISOR'S NOTES

The script supervisor's report summarizes the shooting day, giving a detailed account of which scenes were shot that day and how many scenes are left to complete. The script notes are a line-by-line account of the coverage that was shot for each scene and which action and dialogue was covered by each camera. The script notes from the day accompany the film that will be sent to the editors. A copy of the notes goes with all this other paperwork to the production office. If there is not a copy machine in the production trailer, you may have to go to a local copy store to make copies for the editors and for the production office. Listen very carefully to the script supervisor's instructions. Their documentation is very important and they usually have a particular way they like to handle their paperwork.

LUNCH COUNT

This form comes from the caterer and tells how many people were served lunch for that day.

LUNCH REPORT

At lunch, someone should call in the lunch report to the production office. This lets them know which scenes have been completed and which haven't. It helps them keep the rest of the world informed.

WRAP REPORT

At wrap, the production office submits a wrap report to the studio to keep them informed about the production's progress.

START PAPERWORK OR CONTRACTS

Some individuals who work only one or two days may not have filled out their paperwork before showing up at the set. In this case they will need their start package or contract. Once this paperwork is filled out, return it to the production office ASAP.

Scheduling Paperwork

The following describes important pieces of paperwork that you will use or come across every day on your production. These are not items that go into the daily pouch.

SCHEDULING TOOLS

There are several scheduling systems for getting a film shot on time and in an orderly manner—these systems range from completely hand done to completely computerized. Most production people today use a combination of hand work and computer work.

BREAKING IT DOWN

When a UPM or 1st AD is hired to work on a project, one of the first things he does is break down the script. Breaking down the script involves taking each line of the script and asking who, what, when, where, how. For example: What kinds of guns are in this scene? Will the guns fire? Is there water in the bathtub? Do we need smoke? Is the fire burning in the fire place? Is this with the real dog or the robotic dog? Is she smoking a cigar? How many extra aliens will be needed? Will this be with the green slime or the blue slime? The 1st AD discusses these questions in detail during pre-production with the director and UPM. From those answers, the 1st fills in a form for each scene that details what is required from each department. This form is called a breakdown sheet. Translating these questions into answers gives you a skeleton schedule.

THE PRODUCTION BOARD

Once the script is broken down, the 1st AD or UPM creates the production board—again, either manually or electronically. The production board is composed of long strips of paper that contain information about each scene. For example: scene number, breakdown sheet number, interior or exterior, day or night, set name, cast members who work in the scene, scene descriptions are all items usually included on the strips. The strips of paper fit inside long plastic strips that come in different colors. The colors correspond to where and when a scene takes place: Interior Day = Yellow; Exterior Day = Green; Interior Day = White; Exterior Day = Blue. The 1st AD or UPM arranges, and rearranges, the strips to create a schedule that is workable for all. When sorting and arranging the strips, the following variables are taken into consideration: feature film versus television project; locations; interiors versus exteriors; days versus nights; special effects; weather constraints; kids and animals; availability of key cast or crew members; budget restrictions.

SHOOTING SCHEDULE

Once the production board is completed, the 1st AD or UPM generates the printed shooting schedule. This multi-page form lists all the information that was input onto the breakdown sheets, and organizes it in such a way that each department can figure out specifically what is needed for each scene.

ONE-LINE SCHEDULE

The one-line schedule is an abbreviated version of the full shooting schedule. It is less detailed than the full shooting schedule and is easier for the crew to work with on a daily basis. It still shows the shooting day number, the scenes to be shot, the actors required, and any special requirements from the various departments.

DAY-OUT-OF-DAYS

A day-out-of-days is a form that graphs the working schedule of each actor hired on the show. It indicates their separate start days, work days, hold days, and finish work days, as well as travel days and holidays. It also tallies the total amount of days the actor will work for the run of the show. [Note: The computerized scheduling programs also allow you to create day-out-of-day forms for each separate department. This can be quite useful if you have many different vehicles, for example, and need a detailed sheet showing which vehicle works when].

Miscellaneous Paperwork

PETTY CASH (PC)

Petty cash is money lent, or floated, to you by production to pay for incidental expenses that you incur on behalf of the production. If you carry petty cash, make sure you have an organized system for keeping track of your receipts and accounting for the cash. If the production gives you petty cash, keep it in a separate envelope from your money. When you buy things for the production, make sure to get a receipt showing the name of the business (or vendor), the date of the expenditure and the amount paid.

If someone wants to borrow money from your petty cash, you will need to sign it out to them by creating an IOU for the amount of money lent. When that person gives you the receipt for the items bought with your petty cash, then give them back their IOU slip. This way you will not forget where all your money has gone. Once you have spent your petty cash, collect any outstanding IOUs or receipts. Tape all your receipts to a sheet of paper and number them. Log them on the petty cash form and add up the amount. Make a copy of the log and receipts (for your records) and turn the originals into accounting. If all your paperwork is in order, they should reimburse you fairly quickly.

Part IV

"Once I was in charge of keeping an eye on a famous old-time actor while we waited for the camera department to finish setting up the shot. It was a cold, windy day and we were in the middle of the plains with dust and tumble weeds whipping around us. The actor sat in a heated car, staying warm and resting. He beckoned to me and told me to sit in the back of his car. As I sat there, warm for the first time in hours, he sang me an old shipmate's song.

I went straight from that warm, fuzzy experience back to base camp where the 2nd 2nd AD and I dodged cell phones as they rocketed out of an actress' trailer. Unfortunately, our location had little or no phone reception.

It's like anything else in life. Some people remember where they have been and how they got there and others . . . well, I guess they conveniently forget.

April

10

The Cast

THE PRINCIPALS

Sometimes on a film you will have little contact with the principal actors and sometimes you may have a bit more contact. In any case, it's good to be prepared once you do start working with actors on a day-to-day basis. When the actors for a film are cast, they sign a contract that has certain negotiated perks (size and kind of trailer, specific makeup person and/or hairdresser, certain working hours, etc.) Usually the 2nd 2nd AD runs base camp. If you are helping to run base camp you will become very aware of their perks and their personalities. Actors usually are highly sensitive individuals. Each show is different. Sometimes you will have the good fortune to work with actors who not only are talented but are nice people as well. Sometimes you will work with those who are completely absorbed in themselves. It is a lonely, fishbowl world with people pressing their noses up against the glass. Give them their space. If they need you, they'll let you know.

DAY PLAYERS

Day players may be big stars *(cameos)* or not such big stars, *(up-and-comer)*. If you are assisting the 2nd 2nd AD in base camp, the day players can sneak up on you on the call sheet if you are not paying attention. If you practice that good habit of reading the call sheet and scenes every day before work, you will have no problem. Sometimes there will not be a room for them in base camp and everyone has to scramble in the morning to find room in the trailers. Day players will usually sign their *SAG contract* on the day that they work. The production office will usually send the contracts out to the AD department on the set. If you are on a nonunion show and are running base camp you will need to make sure the office sends out the paper work on the day for your day players. They may only work one day on the entire film so make sure their paper work is handled on *that* day. This goes for *stunties* (stunt day players) too. The actress should fill out her paperwork which should be included in the *nightly pouch* to the office.

STAR TREATMENT

Certain stars are accustomed to being treated a certain way. Some stars surround themselves with their entourage; others will be totally obscure and the only time you will see them is when they come to the set. When dealing with stars, I think it is best to treat them as you would treat everyone else, because they are like everyone else.

Pay attention to their needs. Keep them warm, fed, dry and away from pesky people. Keep a set of sides handy in case they forget theirs. Keep water nearby and remember their favorite snacks. Do not sit in their chair—or anyone's chair—ever.

During emotional or violent scenes, keep your distance. Actors have to get all worked up for heavy duty scenes and you do not want to break their concentration.

AGENTS

When agents visit, they come to see their clients (the actors and actresses) and see that they are being treated well. Point them in the direction of their client, the phone and fax machine, and they will be fine.

THE STUDIO

Every so often the executives from the studio ("the suits") will make an appearance on the set. You will be able to spot them a mile away. They are usually in business suits standing amazed at how dirty and busy we all look. Treat them the same way you do the actors. Find them a chair to sit in and make sure they know where the phone and fax machines are.

These are the folks that *green-light* and *red-light* pictures every day. They write checks for millions and millions of dollars. They are the investors and they like to come out to the field to see how their investment is doing. People on the crew may get a little uptight when they are around because everyone likes to look good and strut their stuff. Do not get in the way. Smile, listen and learn.

EXTRAS

If you are working in LA, people can do extra work full time and make a living at it. Most of them are regulars and you will get to know them. They are used to the routine and know how a set runs. Out of town, it will more than likely be a first time experience and one they will never forget. If you give them information about how the set works and how long they may have to wait, you will have a good bunch. Have fun. If you make it fun for them and keep them included in what is going on, hopefully they will enjoy themselves. Making movies should be fun for everyone involved.

11

The Crew

This is a list of the crew and a little synopsis of what each person does. However, no one's job can be this simplified. I have listed them in the rough order that they appear on the call sheet. It is a good idea to familiarize yourself with where everyone is listed. Some jobs are not listed on the call sheet so I have listed them around the department that they usually deal with the most.

DIRECTOR

Responsible for translating the written word into the visual medium. The director's vision of the film guides what the final product will be in terms of look, feel and sound. Many times, the screenwriter and the director are the same.

SCREENWRITER

Responsible for the telling the story. Sometimes present on the set for revisions and story integrity. Without the screenwriter, there would be no screenplay and, therefore, no movie.

EXECUTIVE PRODUCER

They are attached to the project either because they own the rights or they found the story, or they have been hired by the studio to oversee the project. Sometimes it's part of another crew member's deal to get a producing credit.

PRODUCER

Develops the project and screenplay into a workable shooting script. Instrumental in bringing the optimum cast and crew together.

LINE PRODUCER

The line producer is responsible for bringing the project in on time and on budget. They make most of the spending and logistical decisions on the set. Ideally, they help the director get what he or she wants. It is not their job to be liked. Their job is to oversee how the money is spent. On films with smaller budgets the line producer and UPM will be the same person.

UNIT PRODUCTION MANAGER

The unit production manager (UPM) signs most of the checks and money requests. Has an intimate knowledge of every single line of the budget. The UPM hires and fires crew members; and approves schedules, call sheets and production reports.

1ST ASSISTANT DIRECTOR

First ADs are in charge of running the set. They are responsible for keeping a certain pace during shooting. They communicate to the crew what is happening and what will happen. They also conduct *safety meetings*. With input from the producers, the UPM and the director, the 1st AD creates the shooting schedule. They are responsible for making any schedule changes and for keeping the show on schedule. They oversee and direct the background artists.

2ND ASSISTANT DIRECTOR

The second assistant director makes sure that everyone has a call time and knows when and where to be at work. He sets the background; prepares the call sheet; disseminates information from 1st AD to AD team and the rest of the crew. In general, 2nd ADs have to be great communicators.

2ND 2ND ASSISTANT DIRECTOR

Second 2nd assistant directors are in charge of getting the actors through hair and makeup and ready for the set. In other words, he helps them get ready for the camera. He runs base camp and prepares the production report.

SET PA

Says "YES."

PRODUCTION OFFICE COORDINATOR (POC)

The production office coordinator (POC) is a direct link to the UPM and usually works as the UPM's right hand. The POC runs the production office. They are one of the first crew members to be hired, and one of the last to finish. A great resource, they filter all the paperwork that one production generates. They can answer most of your questions and are an integral part of any production. They handle phones, pagers, rooms, travel arrangements, crew lists, deliveries, film shipments, copiers, time cards, out times, Fed Ex, call sheets, wrap reports, dailies and wrap beer. They can be a fabulous support system.

ASSISTANT PRODUCTION OFFICE COORDINATOR (APOC)

The assistant POC is the POC's right hand person. Often they have responsibility over a certain area, such as handling all travel arrangements.

PRODUCTION SECRETARY

Usually in charge of distribution of printed matter, the production secretary has great phone etiquette and great copying skills.

OFFICE PA

Assists the production office staff with whatever needs doing. This is also a great entry level position as well as a great place to learn about the different departments.

ACCOUNTING

The money folks. The number crunchers. Do your time card and remind the crew to do theirs. Turn your petty cash in on time and this gang will love you.

SCRIPT SUPERVISOR

This very meticulous and detail-conscious person keeps track of all things that happen during each shot. The script supervisor also tallies all coverage that is done for each scene. She maintains a log of what scenes are still owed; times the length of each shot; and makes sure the continuity is maintained from scene to scene. She also notes if the actors change any dialogue during the scene.

DIRECTOR OF PHOTOGRAPHY (DP)

Also called the cinematographer, the DP is responsible for the overall look of the film. He coordinates with the director and the camera crew. He gives them the f-stop and light readings. He also choreographs the shot with the director. He works closely with the head electrician (gaffer) to get the best lighting arrangement for the scene.

CAMERA OPERATOR

The operator is the crew member who puts his eye to the viewfinder and shoots. His view through the lens of the scene helps with the choreography of the shot.

FIRST ASSISTANT CAMERA

His job is to make sure the camera is in focus during the shot.

SECOND ASSISTANT CAMERA

He begins (or ends) each scene by clapping the slate (AKA sticks) on which is written information about the production, the director, the producer, the scene number and the take. Helps make focus marks. Helps measure the distance between the subject and the camera.

LOADER

This camera crewperson loads new *magazines* (AKA canisters) of film into the camera. He also unloads the used film and packs it to be shipped to the lab. It is his job to keep track of all the film that the production has used.

STILL PHOTOGRAPHER

She captures the action of the film, the actors and crew with a still camera. [Note: On union films no one is permitted to photograph the action *except* the still photographer].

GAFFER (CHIEF LIGHTING TECHNICIAN)

The head electrician (AKA the gaffer) who coordinates with the DP to create the shadows and light for the film. He is the head of the electric department and oversees the crew of electricians.

KEY GRIP

It is the key grip's responsibility to work with the gaffer and the DP to rig, support, flag and otherwise facilitate the shot. Grips are usually the strongest men and women on the set.

BEST BOY

Although this job often goes to a woman and is officially known as "assistant chief lighting technician" or "assistant key grip," the common name for the job is "best boy." He or she is second in command to the gaffer or the key grip.

DOLLY GRIP

A member of the camera department, dolly grips are in charge of moving the dolly on which the camera sits for a certain kind of tracking shot.

ELECTRICIAN

Under the direction of the chief lighting technician (the gaffer) these crew members provide the lights, set them up (rig) and dismantle (strike) them.

GRIP

These strong crew members rig, lift, haul, lug, and many other things involved in setting up for a shot.

SOUND MIXER

This person is responsible for the capturing production sound of the movie. Sometimes they park themselves as far as their cords will reach so as to be away from the hustle and bustle of setting up the shot. Often they attach small microphones with battery packs to actors in order to capture sound that might otherwise be impossible to record. The sound mixer often uses a *comtech*—a device that enables the sound mixer and other crew members to hear what the actors are saying. Sometimes you will need a comtech for cueing the background.

BOOM OPERATOR

This is the person who holds the microphone on a long pole called the *boom*. They hold the boom as close to the actors as possible, without letting the microphone drop into the shot. They have strong arms!

VIDEO ASSIST

This person provides video playback at *video village* for the director and DP. This way they can see what they are about to shoot or what they have just shot. The video cables attach directly into the camera.

PRODUCTION DESIGNER

The head of the art department who is responsible for coordinating the overall look of the film according to the director's vision. He works closely with the director when choosing locations and deciding upon set design.

ART DIRECTOR

The second in command of the art department (and often the head of the art department on smaller budget pictures), the art director does most of the hands-on designing of the sets. The art director works hand-in-hand with the production designer and the director.

SET DECORATOR

The member of the art department who acquires all the materials needed for the set (couches, dishes, paintings, photographs, clothes in the closet, coasters, candlesticks, and so forth).

SET DRESSER

Responsible to the set decorator, the on-set dresser takes care of the items that were acquired for the set. If the items need to be polished or aged, it is the set dresser's responsibility.

ART DEPARTMENT

The art department is composed of the production designer, the art director, the set decorator, the set dresser, the drafters, the artists, and others. For production assistants wanting to work in a physically creative area, being a set PA in the art department is a good place to start.

ON-SET PAINTER (STANDBY PAINTER)

These crew members paint anything needing painting. Sometimes there is a spot that is causing a glare on the camera and they have to eliminate the glare with dulling spray.

PROPERTY MASTER

The property master is in charge of all items that an actor picks up and uses in a scene. Props can include coffee mugs, spectacles, cameras, fans, saddles, rings, watches, as well as all food that the actors eat during the scene.

KEY HAIRSTYLIST

These crew members are in charge of giving actors a particular "look" for the film, and for maintaining that look throughout each shooting day.

KEY MAKEUP ARTIST

This crew member works to give the performers their special makeup "look" for the film, and for maintaining it each shooting day.

COSTUME DESIGNER

The costume designer works with the director as well as the production designer to create a style of dress for each character. Many times this means having each piece of clothing designed and fabricated. Other times, it means coordinating buying the appropriate clothes.

WARDROBE SUPERVISOR

The wardrobe supervisor oversees the clothing. They also are instrumental in purchasing the necessary clothes for the actors. If you are cold, they can loan you a jacket and if you rip your jeans running after some dog that is about to walk into the shot, they always have safety pins.

SET COSTUMER

Handles the actors' clothing while on the set. Checks them immediately before the camera rolls.

GREENSPERSON

Handle any trees or greens that need to be added or subtracted from a shot. Also, if you need a chain saw, this is the place.

CARPENTERS

These members of the construction crew build anything that needs to be built.

SPECIAL FX

These specialized crew members build and control any special effect (smoke, steam, fire, snow, ice, explosions, breakaway glass, rain, wind, fake walls, bombs, sparks and so forth). Often times they are part of a team or group from a separate company that has been hired to do all the special effects (mechanical or physical).

MECHANICAL AND/OR PHYSICAL FX

These FX crew members are in charge of building anything needed in the way of physical and/or mechanical special effects. Some examples are: collapsible bridges, anything mechanical with motor parts, and some animatronics, miniatures, robotics and puppets.

VISUAL FX

The magic of movie making happens quite often here. Need a canyon, skyscraper, volcano, star ship fleet, large audience or just your basic run-of-the-mill ICBM explosion? Okay! Bring in the visual FX team. They start with little or nothing in terms of images and, with computer graphics, virtually create something out of thin air—or thin microchips, anyway. Visual FX also covers blue screen, green screen, motion control, rear screen projection, miniatures, composites, computer graphics and plate shots. The future is here. They make it far more interesting!

EDITOR

Editors can and have played a very big role in the final version of a picture. It is a fascinating career and there are some very good books written regarding editing, should you decide to pursue this avenue. The editor harmoniously pieces together the story by taking all the raw footage and assembling it either on film or digitally.

ASSISTANT EDITOR

This member of the editing team logs and tracks all the raw footage and helps the editor assemble the film.

LOCATION MANAGER

This is one of the very first people hired on a project as prep begins. After reading the script and reviewing the budget, the *location manager* or *location scout* looks for the most ideal location to shoot each scene. Once the director has chosen his locations, the Locations Department makes the maps and signs that lead to the location. They are the liaisons between the community and the film company, and are amazing diplomats.

TRANSPORTATION COORDINATOR

The transportation coordinator is the boss of the transportation department. He is responsible for making sure all the vehicles end up in the right place at the right time.

TRANSPORTATION CAPTAIN

The captain is the on-set boss and is responsible for the logistics and flow of vehicles, trailers and drivers. These drivers work hard. Be good to these people and they will take care of you. When you are fast asleep, these folks are up moving the trailers so you will have a place to prepare your call sheet later in the day. And after you are tucked in your bed they are still moving trucks and equipment.

PICTURE CAR COORDINATOR

This member of the transportation department is in charge of all the *picture cars* that are used in the movie.

WRANGLER

Any and all animals used in the movie will need a wrangler. There is usually a special wrangler for each type of animal. Horse wrangler, moth wrangler, beaver wrangler, spider wrangler, camel wrangler.

ANIMAL TRAINER

Animal trainers work with animals that have been trained specifically for filmmaking. These trainers handle more than the average cats and dogs—they handle rats, baboons, birds, snakes, cheetahs, and more.

HUMANE SOCIETY REPRESENTATIVE

This representative from the Humane Society is present whenever you are working with animals. Their presence helps make sure that the animals receive proper care and handling.

STUNT COORDINATOR

Usually a member of the Screen Actors Guild, the stunt coordinator is in charge of designing, choreographing and running all stunt sequences. All the stunt performers on a show will report to the stunt coordinator. It is not unusual in a big action picture for the stunt coordinator also to be the second unit director.

STUNT PEOPLE

The people with enough fear to understand how dangerous what they are doing is.

CATERER

Mmmmmm. Where would we be without these people? Boy, is it nice to have a good hot meal after a grueling day of work.

CRAFT SERVICE

This is where the crew finds itself snacking between meals. Find out what your ADs favorite snacks are and make sure that the craft service person keeps them stocked. Nothing worse than a hungry AD . . . except a hungry and wet AD with a dead battery.

MEDIC

The medic, or first aid person, takes care of all your bumps, scrapes, headaches, red eyes, sniffles, sneezes, coughs and other ailments. They are also proficient in CPR.

EXTRAS COORDINATOR

This person, or firm, is responsible for hiring and tracking all the extras needed for the film. These folks have a great eye for "real people."

ACTING COACH

This acting teacher spends time with the actors rehearsing lines or developing their specific character.

STUDIO TEACHER

Studio teachers (AKA Welfare Workers) are required by law to be on the set every day when child actors under a certain age are working. The children are required by law to have a minimum amount of daily schooling. There are very specific guidelines governing work hours and school hours for child actors.

TECHNICAL ADVISOR

These specialists provide detailed and accurate information on specific careers that may be explored in the film. Military advisors, butterfly specialists, volcanologists, ballerinas, astronauts, marine biologists, inmates, heart surgeons and pianists are all examples of technical advisors.

PUBLICIST

Often left out on smaller pictures due to budgetary limitations, a good publicist can be extremely instrumental in getting good press for a picture. They work with the local and international press and know them well. A good publicist functions as a liaison between the local community and the production. They schedule press conferences and visits to the set by members of the press. They provide the studio with updates from location as well as prepare all the press materials needed for the show.

ELECTRONIC PRESS KIT (EPK) CREW

The Electronic Press Kit people shoot video of the behind-the-scenes work and interview the key players. This footage is then used in all the news clips right before the movie opens.

POLICE OFFICERS AND FIRE FIGHTERS

You will usually find police and fire officials present at every set in a busy area or during fire or traffic sequences.

They will help make your life easier, particularly when you are having to stop traffic or clear an area away due to a big special effects sequence.

DIRECTOR'S AND PRODUCER'S ASSISTANTS

These assistants make the lives of the director and the producer(s) a little easier. Although it sometimes seems as if they are keeping you away from their bosses, they are in effect taking care of all the small details that would prevent their bosses from the job at hand—making the movie! Anything that needs to go to the producer or director should go through their assistants and not directly to them.

SAFETY CONSULTANT

This crew member oversees all safety procedures on the set, inspects sets and locations for safety hazards.

AERIAL COORDINATOR

Coordinates any flying activity to be used during filming.

MARINE COORDINATOR

Similar to the air coordinator, the marine coordinator is in charge of all work done on the water as well as water-going vessels.

The crew members listed above are primarily part of the active production. Development and post-production personnel go beyond the scope of this book.

12

Background (Extras)

WHAT IS BACKGROUND?

Background or *Extras* (or *Atmosphere*) are people whose presence on screen makes the film appear more like real life. For example, when you stand on a street corner, people usually cross in front of you and behind you on their way to wherever they are going. Background serves this same purpose. Extras fill in the shot and create movement and life in a scene and can add some nice moments to a lifeless frame. There are times when background is inappropriate (i.e., love scenes, intense dialogue scenes, monologues).

WHERE DO EXTRAS COME FROM?

Extras come from all walks of life. An *extras casting company* is usually hired to cast the appropriate extras for the film. Each film has a different look and different needs so the casting company will hire the right people for the film. The production company pays the extras casting company who, in turn, then pays the extras. If there are more than a few extras working, a representative from the extras casting company will help with the additional work.

WHO ARE THESE EXTRAS?

People often take work as an extra to get started in acting or because they enjoy working in and around the filmmaking process. Some have been doing it for years and others only a few days. It can be a tough road as an extra. The pay is low, the hours are long and there is a lot of sitting around waiting to be called in to do a scene. Extras are hired by an extras casting company that deals specifically with providing background artists. Some people take extra work as their primary source of income like the extras in LA. However, outside LA, many extras are retirees and business people. They take the job because a film has come to their town and they want to participate. Be conscious of this. Respect their interest in the business either way. It is fulfilling to get to know your extras. It is also helpful to learn their names so that when the ADs call for them, you know almost all them and can help the ADs when they have to start shuffling them around.

A LITTLE BACK STORY

When a movie is in pre-production, the director and the 1st AD discuss the background needs for each scene. Each film has different background needs. Some films by the nature of the script will have little or no background. Some films have a few thousand extras. If there are a lot of extras in a movie, more PA jobs are available—good! Some directors like to have a lot of extras and others prefer only a few. The 1st AD and the extras casting company discuss and decide upon the number and kind of extras that the casting company will need to provide. The casting company then begins work immediately securing the needed extras.

HOW DO YOU FIT IN?

Usually a PA is placed with the extras to put them through the works. If you get this job, embrace it. It is valuable to the ADs to know there is someone reliable with the extras who will have them ready by the time the camera is ready to shoot. On bigger shows, a person from extras casting will work with the set PAs as well as assist with the additional work.

EXTRA! EXTRA! READ ALL ABOUT IT!

Usually the routine goes something like this: Justin Thyme signs up to be an extra in a movie that has come to his town. He is cast by extras casting, goes into wardrobe for a fitting and goes home. The day before Justin's scene arrives, extras casting or the 2nd AD calls him with a call time for the next day. On the big day he shows up on time at the location. He gets in a shuttle with the other 100 extras who are also in the scene. They arrive in a large group, check in, fill out their *vouchers* (time cards), go through wardrobe, hair, makeup and props. Then they proceed to the extras holding area and wait to be called onto the set to do a scene. After all 100 are ready, the 1st or 2nd AD will come in, read the scene to the extras, and then describe what the extras are to do in the scene. Once the camera is ready the 1st AD will call for a certain number of extras. Justin Thyme is selected as part of a group which walks onto the set. He is then given his particular action by the 1st or 2nd AD. He is to walk from here to there and back to here again. On the way from here to there he stops to talk to a woman coming out of a hat shop. When they talk they will *mime* so that it does not disrupt the scene with the principal actors. This is Justin's *"bit of business."* He fits into the scene and does not stand out. If the background artist stands out, then he defeats the purpose. This is why it is called background, not foreground. The crew finishes the scene and the extras are excused. It's time to go home. Justin packs up his playing cards and premed homework. He returns his clothes to wardrobe and his gun to props and signs out with extras casting and the PAs. Once the extras are gone, you and another PA will compile the extras' paperwork. That is the basic routine.

SETTING UP

The call time for the extras varies. Usually they arrive early so that they can be ready on time. Post signs directing the extras to check-in, holding, wardrobe, the changing rooms, and the bathrooms. Before the extras arrive, make sure you have enough extras vouchers and pens for them to use when signing in.

VOUCHERS

When the extras arrive, the first thing they will do is fill out their *voucher.* Extras are paid by the extras casting company. Therefore, they need proof of work in order to be paid. This proof is the voucher that is basically their time card. When an extra gives you his name, you will find it on the list and give him a voucher. It's nice to have a filled out voucher taped to the table or posted as an example of how to fill it out properly in order to expedite the process. He should fill it out thoroughly. Once he fills out his voucher, he should hold onto it and proceed to extras holding.

SKINS

As the extras arrive, check their names off the *skins*—a list of the extras that are due to work that day. It is generated by the extras casting company. The names are listed alphabetically or numerically. It is faxed or delivered to the production office the day before the extras are scheduled to shoot. If you have a large group of extras, the casting company may have given each extra a separate number. Each extra will give you their number rather than their name when they check in.

THE COUNT

Once the crowd around check-in dies down, count the number of extras who checked in and see if any are missing. Give the 2nd AD a count of how many are present and how many are still missing. The extras coordinator will call the ones who have not arrived.

THE WORKS

Now that you have most of the extras, go to the holding area and begin sending them through the works (hair, makeup, wardrobe and props). If you have a large group, take them to the various departments in small manageable groups.

WARDROBE

Most of the extras are fitted for their wardrobe before the day of the shoot. On the day(s) of the shoot, those extras will proceed directly to wardrobe, change into their outfit, and put their own clothes back into extras holding. [Note: Get them dressed first so they will not ruin their hairstyle when changing clothes.] On period films you may have to help wardrobe tie corsets, help props hand out guns, or help makeup apply dirt. If you have a large group to get through wardrobe, talk to the wardrobe team and see what works best for them. Form organized lines and keep a path clear for the crew who needs to pass through. Sometime two lines work better with men in one and women in the other. After dressing, the extras then go to hair and makeup.

HAIR AND MAKEUP

Period films can be particularly challenging if there are many extras who need their hair and makeup done. Hair can take a long time. Try to create a system. Monitor a line. As soon as one person is out of the hair chair and done then another one should be ready to sit down. You would be surprised how much faster it will go if you are there making sure the chairs are always filled. On a big show you may have 15 or 20 hair people! Try to meet all them and offer to bring them coffee or water. They are stuck in that room until all the hair is finished. For most extras, very little makeup is required. The makeup department might give them a *once over* or a *makeup blessing*. Once finished with hair and makeup, the extras will return to holding to stand by for shooting.

HOLDING

Extras Holding should be a clean and well-ventilated area. Sometimes Holding will be next to the set, in which case you should be aware of the potential noise problem. In Holding, there should be water, coffee and some snacks. It should be a place where they can hang out, play cards, read and wait until they are needed on set. Usually there will be a PA planted near extras holding to gather them quickly when they are needed on the set. Make sure you have some bathrooms set aside as well. Ask the extras to let you or another PA know if they are going to use the bathroom or go out for a smoke. This way you will know where to find them if they are needed. If you have a large group, you may need to split them up by the first letter of their last name, by their numbers or by birthdays. To keep a large group attentive it helps to hold a drawing or raffle to keep the day moving along (especially if there is a lot of waiting).

BACKGROUND ACTION

Once the extras are called to the set, the 1st AD will outline what she would like to see, based on her conversation with the director. The 2nd AD will start to lay in the background, giving each extra a *bit of business* (motivation for what they have been doing and where they are going). On DGA shows, the 1st and 2nd ADs set the background. If you are working on a nonunion show, you may get to set some background. If so, try giving each extra a bit of business. If the extra is going to walk from one street corner to the next, give them a reason for doing it (for example, it is their Aunt's birthday and they need to pick up a cake at the bakery). Give everyone something to do and they will inevitably feel as if they are contributing to the film. If it is a DGA show, you will assist the 2nd AD in bringing the correct amount of people from extras holding to the set. You will also keep track of who is who, and what extras are missing.

Most background action concerns crossing through the frame (for example: past a window, across a street, cars crossing, a group of school kids). Once the camera is ready, the actors have rehearsed, and the background is set— you will shoot. Background action starts before the main action starts. The activity in the scene is up and bustling by the time the principals begin. There are some general rules that seem to work with setting background. If you are on a nonunion show and get to participate you may find a few of these tips helpful.

BACKGROUND TIPS

- **Know what the shot is and what the frame lines are.**

- **Keep track of who is where.** Make sure you know where everyone is going so you do not end up with a cluster of people on one side of the camera or a blank spot in the frame on the other.

- **Give delayed cues.** This means that if five extras start off screen, start one person right on the background action cue; another two, five seconds later; the other three, ten seconds after that. You can also cue your extras to begin once a piece of action has occurred. For example, "Once the burning car passes in front of you, run across the street to the telephone booth." Keep it simple!

- **Rotate the background in a circle, triangle or square if you have an extremely long scene.**

- **Learn the names of the extras and know their action.** Try to take a Polaroid® of the extras who are in the foreground or very close to the camera. If the scene continues later on in the film, it is very important to know if an extra who figured prominently in today's scene will be available to work three weeks from now when that subsequent scene is shot. [Note: On union films, you will not be allowed to take the photograph. Ask the still photographer to take a few for you.]

- **Make a map.** It's good to make a diagram on the back of your sides or in your notebook of who is where for any future references and, of course, for matching. Matching is important once the director starts to shoot the coverage. The extras will need to repeat their actions in the same manner over and over again. Otherwise there may be a problem with *continuity*.

- **Work out a system of silent cues.** Most of the time, all the background will move on *"background action"* but there are exceptions. Silent cues can be a point or a tap on the shoulder. If you give a silent cue, make sure they can see you and that each extra understands their cue.

- **Break your extras into ones and threes, as well as couples.** Often, the background action in a movie looks odd if there are too many couples.

- **Make sure that the background action does not get in the way of the main action and the actors in the scene.**

- **An extra should *never* look at the camera, unless instructed to by the 1st AD or the Director.**

CHECK OUT

Once the extras are released, a PA shuttles them to the various departments to return the gear (wardrobe, guns, watches, hairpiece, scars) they were given at the start of the day. Once they have returned everything and turn in their vouchers, they are free to leave. They will bring their vouchers to you to sign out. It will have their check in time and check out time. A representative from the extras casting company will usually be present to assist with check out. After the extra has turned in his voucher, he is excused. Once you have collected all the vouchers from the day, you need to organize them chronologically. The vouchers are then counted and logged by the times the extras arrived and departed and whether they are SAG or nonunion extras. These numbers are transcribed onto the *extras report.* The numbers from your tabulation should be included in production report. Put the vouchers into an envelope for the accounting department with a tally of the numbers from the day or a copy of the extras report.

This paperwork goes with the nightly pouch to the production office. Below is an example of a typical extras report:

# EXTRAS	IN	OUT	LUNCH	AMT
10 SAG	0700	1700	1/2 HR	$100/DAY
70 NON UNION	0700	1900	1/2 HR	$55/DAY
20 SAG	0700	1930	1/2 HR	$100/DAY

[Note: Screen Actors Guild (SAG) extras are paid differently from the nonunion extras. Extras are eligible for membership after a certain amount of days worked as an extra. Check SAG rules for current criteria.]

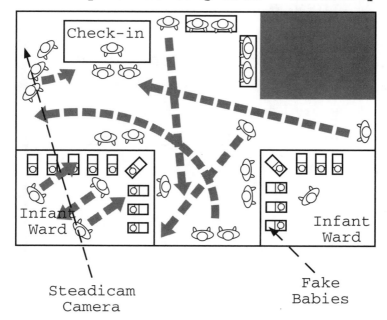

Background diagram

"I was walking down the street in Dallas and I got shuffled into a large group of people. They happened to be extras in a movie and they thought I was an extra. They fed me and treated me well. I asked people all day what they did and did they enjoy their work? Everyone seemed pleased and happy and they wore shorts. I decided then that I would work in the film business and here I am!"

Tina Stauffer
2nd Assistant Director
Dante's Peak, Wyatt Earp,
Heaven And Earth, The Little Princess

13

Stand-Ins (Second Team)

WHAT DOES A STAND-IN DO?

A *stand-in's* job (also known as *second team*) is twofold. First, they help the director of photography and gaffer line up and light the scene while the actor is getting ready. Second, they allow the actor time to get into hair, makeup and wardrobe for their scene. The stand-in is present at the rehearsals to learn the blocking of "their actor." Once the scene is blocked, the actors go back to get ready, while the crew lights the scene. A stand-in usually resembles the actor in terms of height and build, hair color and skin tone. A stand-in wears similar clothes to "their actor." They stand where the actor would stand while the crew lights around them.

PROXIMITY TO THE SET

The stand-ins should be just off the set, not too far yet not too close. They should know to watch the rehearsals and *stand by* to step in once the actors leave to get ready. Keep an eye on your second team and establish a relationship. They can help you. Let them know that you need them to stay close and if they want to step away from the set, they should let you or one of the PAs or ADs know.

CHECK IN

As the stand-ins arrive they should check in with the AD department, get a voucher, have some breakfast and go straight to wardrobe. Since there is almost always a rehearsal when you start a new location or set, make sure you are there to welcome them and tell them where the rehearsal is being held.

CHECK OUT

Stand-ins usually wrap when the actors they have been standing-in for wrap. Sometimes they will be kept for an off-camera eyeline, but usually they will be wrapped when the actor is wrapped. Make sure you note their out times and collect their vouchers.

14

Helping Out

Between shots, there is a lot of equipment to be torn down (disassembled), moved and setup. Make yourself useful and helpful.

MOVING STUFF

Once the camera angle changes positions it is called a *new deal.* Everything that once was not seen in the shot, is now visible in the shot. The equipment, bodies and paraphernalia must be moved. Make sure your help is actually needed before you assist someone with moving their stuff. The crew can get very territorial about gear and, although you are trying to help, save yourself the anxiety by talking to them beforehand. Simply say, "The camera is looking this way now. Is there anything I can help you move?"

PULLING CABLE

Sometimes there will be a long tracking shot and the camera department will need one or two people to pull up the slack in the cable as the camera dollies backwards or forwards. If you get to pull cable, stay alert and on your toes otherwise you will find yourself all knotted up with cable around your ankles, not to mention being totally embarrassed!

CLEANING UP

It's nice to help keep the area you are shooting in clean. If you see trash, pick it up.

WRANGLING

Keep an eye and ear on the talent, key department heads, or extras or anyone who needs to be found. You do not have to follow them around like a spy, keep an eye on where people go so that when they are needed you can find them. Be conscious of whoever is around you.

PARKING CARS

You may be asked to help park cars if the transportation department is busy. (This will be when you are glad you practiced your parallel parking.)

CRAFT SERVICE

This is where you will find the snacks. It's nice to make the rounds and see if anyone needs anything from Craft Service.

FINDING PEOPLE AND FINDING THINGS

A good friend of mine taught me this very important maneuver. I call it *"Jeffo's Magic 360."* When you are looking for someone, stand in one place and pivot around slowly in a 360-degree circle. As your eyes move through each quadrant, scan the area for whomever you are looking. Most of the time, you will find who or what you were looking for.

UMBRELLAS

Have umbrellas on hand at all times. For rain, or for excessive sun, they are used to shield the actors or key crew as they prepare for the shot or in between takes.

CUEING ACTORS

As you get more experienced on the set, one of your jobs may be to give the actors their cues off screen. This will happen when the camera is located a fair distance from the principal actor. The 1st AD will position a PA with the actor. If the actor and the director need to speak with each other, the PA can facilitate this. Try to let the actor have their space as most of the time they are going over their lines or action in their head. The AD will give you an idea of how he will cue you and then all you need to do is keep your eyes and ears open. You may give the actor a quick point to let him know he is on, or whisper, "Action, Harrison." Sometimes actors prefer to be called by their character's name in which case you would whisper, "Action, Indy."

CUEING CARS

If you are cueing cars through a shot, be careful and stay alert. It can take a while to prepare all the elements for a shot and the people waiting in their cars may fall asleep. Circulate through the cars and let the drivers know what is going on. As you are cueing the cars the AD may tell you on the radio how many cars to send at a particular moment (2-1-3-2-1-3). The AD is right next to the camera or monitor and she can gauge how it is looking—too empty, too busy, or just right.

Part V

"On one of my first PA jobs the 1st AD bellowed at me to go to base camp and get the first team. Eager to please, I raced out to base camp and ran smack into the transportation captain.
I looked up at him desperately. 'Do we have a football team or soccer team out here?' I had no idea what 'first team' meant."

Maggie Murphy
2nd Assistant Director
Dante's Peak, Night Falls On Manhattan,
Nixon, Speed, Blink, Sleepless In Seattle

15

Communications

COMMUNICATING WITH THE CREW

In either your lock up or as you stand by in between set ups it is necessary to share what you hear over the radio with the crew as you receive pertinent information. When the 1st AD tells you to standby, you should echo, loudly, "Standby, please." This gives everyone a chance to get into quiet mode. Then when the 1st AD yells "rolling" you loudly echo "ROLLING!" When the 1st AD lets you know the camera has cut you echo "CUT!" or "CLEAR!" This relaying of information is the only way the crew knows when they can resume whatever it is they are doing. If someone is being noisy, most of the time they do not realize it. Catch their eye and give the ol' shhhhhhhh (but do not shhhh too loud or you'll be the one in the hot box!) Gesture that we are rolling by making a circle in the air with your finger. To indicate we have cut, do the classic "slit your throat" motion. Check out the loud areas before you are rolling then you will be way ahead of the game. There will always be someone who cannot hear himself talking (too many concerts). Just do your best.

IS THERE AN ECHO IN HERE?

The following is a list of some of the lingo used on set. You will hear it over the radio from the 1st or 2nd AD. In turn you should repeat it out loud to the crew around you for optimum communication:

Stand By: We are about to start shooting.

Final Touches: For hair, makeup, and wardrobe this is their last opportunity to look at the actors.

Rehearsing: People should keep the noise down so everyone on the set can hear the blocking instructions, etc. Noise is very distracting to actors when they are rehearsing.

Hold the Work: This means stop hammering on that! It is irritating to everyone on the set.

Holding the Roll: Something has happened to prevent the roll. Resume whatever it is that you were doing.

Make It Safe: This gives whoever is hammering a chance to secure the project he or she is working on and then be quiet.

Rolling: The camera is rolling. There must be absolutely no noise. No cell phones ringing, no sneezing, snickering or beepers beeping.

Fire in the Hole: There will be gunfire in the scene. People should have the option of having some sort of ear protection.

We're Back: Breakfast or lunch is over and it's time to start working.

Lunch 1/2: We are breaking for lunch. You have one-half hour.

Cut or Clear: We've stopped rolling.

That's a Wrap: Everyone's favorite. The day's work is over and it's time to go home.

Calls are Pushed: The call time has been changed.

KILLING THINGS

Sometimes the 1st AD will ask you to *kill* something. Killing something means turning it off or getting rid of some sound or object interrupting the shot. Here is a brief list of things you get to kill:

Kill that Car: Find that car and ask the driver to turn off the engine and lights.

Kill the Condor: Ask Transportation or the Electricians on Channel 3 or 5 to please turn off the condor (giant noisy crane).

Kill the AC: Turn off the air conditioning.

Kill the Playback: Ask the sound person to turn off the playback.

Kill the Smoke: Stop the smoke in the scene (Special Effects *or* FX)

Kill the Blimp: Radio to the blimp in the air that it can stop.

Kill that Extra: Take that extra out of the scene.

You're Killing Me: This means that the 1st AD is ready to slit his wrists because the actors are taking too long to get ready. This is usually followed by a loud groan and another look at his watch.

"Some time ago, I was part
of a small 2nd Unit crew
shooting a horse and
rider. The camera was
across a field and I was
placed near the horse and
rider to cue them. I
tried to speak into my
walkie-talkie to the 1st
AD. Nothing. It was dead.
In a rush to grab all the
equipment, I forgot the
antennas. The 1st AD had
to shout the commands
across the field. I tried
to yell back but then I
startled the horse,
so we used hand signals.
Luckily, they got the
shot and I got to keep
my job."

                    April

16

Radios

Communication

For operations to begin every day, the departments need to be able to communicate with each other. At the shooting location, the production department usually spreads out in order to be most helpful to the crew. So that everyone is not yelling all the time, you use walkie-talkies to communicate. Usually, it is the Production Department's or Sound Department's job to distribute the radios. Almost every department has a walkie-talkie. Some departments have several. Usually every member of the AD department, grip and electric departments carries a walkie. It depends on the budget of the show. If the film can afford a walkie-talkie for almost everyone—great! If not, they will be given to those who need them the most.

Radio Checklist

Your radio is made up of several components. There are two different sizes, but most productions use the smaller walkie-talkies. Once you get your radio, look it over. Familiarize yourself with the features and any accessories that accompany the walkie-talkie. Below is a checklist to walk through as you learn about your radio.

- Antenna—for signal reception (screws on top of the radio)

- Dial—with 6-16 channels
- A switch that can kill interference from other radios in the area (e.g., police)
- PTT button (PTT: Push to talk)
- Speaker—transmits and receives
- Battery—some have different life spans than others
- Battery Charger—a single charger or bank of chargers to replenish the batteries' juice
- Plug—for hand mikes or head sets or both
- Hand Mike—a microphone that attaches to your walkie for ease in talking and responding (Accessory)
- Ear piece—allows you to hear transmissions without open broadcast (Accessory)
- Head Set—a microphone that allows you to transmit and ear piece that allows you to receive transmissions without an open broadcast (Accessory)

Keeping Track of the Radios

RADIO PA

There is usually a PA in charge of the distribution and inventory of the radios. If you get the radio job, figure out a system. Make sure you are organized and can account not only for all the radios, but also for all the accessories as well.

INVENTORY

If you are assigned to the radios, inventory them first thing. Take the list from the rental company and cross check it with the walkie-talkies. Each radio has an inventory number. Once you know you have received all the radios sent, assign the numbered radios to the different departments. Attach a person's name rather than a department to each radio. Distribute the radios to the department with a sign out sheet.

SIGN IN—SIGN OUT

In order to keep track of all the radios, use a *sign out sheet* (see pg. 182). Radios will be either checked out for *run-of-show* or collected each day at wrap. If radios are collected at wrap they will be signed out every day. If a radio is checked out for the duration of the film, then keep the sheet on file. Some departments keep a set of radios for the whole show and return them on the last day with the extra chargers and batteries. Either way, there should be a sign out sheet.

Radios are very expensive. Depending on the brand, they can run as high as $600 each. It is understandable why production managers get very upset if you cannot account for all the radios. It is very easy to lose track of them. When someone wants a radio, they are eager to start their day and they will try to hurry you. TAKE YOUR TIME. Have them sign for the radio. This way they know they are personally responsible if they lose it.

EXAMPLE OF SIGN-OUT SHEET

When you sign out a radio to someone, give that person everything they need to make it work. Put their name, department and the number assigned to the radio on the sheet. You can also label them by department to help you distribute them in the morning. Let them know you will be collecting the radios at wrap so you do not have to go running after their car when they peel out of crew parking.

At the beginning of a show each department will request what radios they need and what accessories they want. Usually grips and electricians need headsets so they can talk hands-free. Each show is different, however. Try to accommodate them. It is the most valuable communication tool on the set.

BATTERIES

Each set of walkie-talkies comes with a bank of chargers. Ideally, you can plug the bank of chargers into one of the trucks (usually the camera truck). Make sure it's a truck that gets power when you wrap. Not all them do. Load up the banks with dead batteries so that there will be charged batteries every morning. Usually one PA is assigned to radios. It is their responsibility to sign them in and out. If this is your job, it is a good idea to bring fresh batteries around periodically. It's a good idea to give both the 1st AD and the 2nd AD new batteries at lunch whether or not they need them. The odds are good that their batteries are almost dead. It saves having to worry about it and it also means their radios will not go dead in the middle of an important discussion.

There are many times during driving, aerial, boating, stunt and animal sequences when radios are imperative to the safety and logistics of getting the shot. Make sure for driving, aerial and stunt shots you have plenty of radios and fresh batteries on hand.

You can tell if someone's battery is dying by a message

that is breaking up or a beep that follows their transmission. If you hear this, do your best to get that person a fresh battery. There is nothing more frustrating than needing to relay some information and being unable to do it because of a dead battery.

Radio Use Guidelines

YOUR RADIO

You are dialed in and have your radio. Let's chat, shall we? There are a few guidelines for effective use of your radio. There is a courteous way to use your radio. There is also a different channel for communication and a language specifically designed for the set.

RADIO ETIQUETTE

Try to count to five before you answer on the radio. Many times, especially when you are eager, you will want to answer a question that has been asked over the radio right away to let people know you have heard the request. If you count to five, hopefully you can prevent *getting stepped on*—having more than one person talk at the same time. It's very annoying and even more frustrating to whoever has asked the question. Also, in your eagerness to respond to the request, you may forget to let the AD or your fellow PAs that you have it handled. An AD says, "Let's bring in the camel wrangler" and you are on the move. You have located the camel wrangler and you are *flying in.* The only thing is, you forgot to tell anyone that you copied the request. Four PAs all fly at the camel wrangler at mach speed. Copy?

CHANNELS

Each radio has several channels. Each department usually has its own channel for communication. They are assigned differently on every show so on the first day try to figure out which department is on each channel.

Channel 1—Production

Channel 2—Used for long conversations/overflow

Channel 3—Open—Stunts or Rigging or Transportation

Channel 4—Transportation or Stunts

Channel 5—Grips

Channel 6—Electricians

Channel 7—Special FX

CHATTER AND LINGO

The best way to use your radio is as little as possible. Listen and learn. Below is a list of things you might hear on the radio to help you communicate a little faster. Remember, it's not a telephone—and everyone can hear what you say.

#1: The first principal actor on the call sheet

#2: The second principal actor on the call sheet

86 It: Forget that request

86 That: Stop that awful noise or turn it off (AKA "Kill That")

Abby Singer: Second to the last shot before wrap

Big 10–4: I copy you

Bogie: Civilian in the shot

Boned: We're dead—we're behind

C–47: Clothes pins

Copy: I understand—I heard you

Final Touches: The vanity team looks at the actors one last time before they go in front of the camera

First Team: The principal actors required for the shot.

Flying In—Speed of light: I'm coming with whatever you requested and I'm moving pretty fast

Flying In: I'm coming with whatever you requested

Go Ahead: Talk to me—I'm listening.

Go to 2: Go to Channel 2—It's not necessary to crowd Channel 1 with my babble

Going 10–100: I am going to the restroom.

Going to 2: Response if someone tells you to go to Channel 2

Hold the Work: Stop that banging please

Holding the Roll: We are waiting to shoot—there is a technical problem

Kill That: Stop that awful noise *or* Turn it off

Last Looks: The vanity team looks at the actors one last time before they go in front of the camera

Lookie-Loo: Civilian in the shot

Lunch 1/2: Lunch has been called for 1/2 hour

Martini: Last shot before wrap

New Deal: New camera setup

On 2: Once you are on 2, let the other party know

On a Bell: Ring the bell to alert everyone that we are about to shoot

Puff and Fluff: Hair, makeup and Wardrobe

Rehearsals Up: We are about to rehearse—quiet please

Rolling: We are rolling film

Roundy Round: The camera angle is turning around 180 degrees

Second Team: The stand-ins

Sides: Pages of the script containing the scenes to be shot that day (usually reduced to a small size)

Skins: A list of the extras for that day of shooting

Stinger: Electrical cord or extension cord

That's a Wrap: You are done with shooting for the day

The Governor: The Director

The Horses Are at the Gate: We are nearing wrap

Vanity Team: Hair, makeup and wardrobe

Watch Your Back: You're about to be hit in the head with something

What's Your 20?: What is your location

COMMUNICATION BREAKDOWN

When the 1st or 2nd AD communicates on the radio, repeat exactly what you hear. Do not interpret and redefine the information. Keep it simple and concise.

TROUBLESHOOTING

Now that you know how to use your walkie, there is a chance something may malfunction. With so many variables, one can only imagine how many things can go wrong. Do not panic. Go through the radio checklist and troubleshoot. Jiggle every part on the list, swear a little, chant to the radio lords, gesture to your fellow PA with a desperate look and shrug. Hopefully, it will start working again and you will look like a genius. If it does not work, flag it with red tape, write "BAD RADIO" on it, and send it back to the production office. They will send it in to the rental company for repair.

LOST AND FOUND

If you or someone on the crew loses your radio and have no idea where it is, report it to the 2nd AD and the production office. Hopefully it will turn up at the end of the show during the inventory. The 2nd AD will note it on the production report.

Essential Calls:

✓ First Shot

✓ Lunch

✓ First Shot After
Lunch

✓ Wrap

17

The Phone

The phone is a necessary tool in the production department when it comes to being the communications link between the production office and the production. Without good communication between the two, there are a million little things that can fall through the cracks.

MANDATORY CALLS

There are a few calls that are essential to keeping the production office and studio informed of the unit's progress. They are basically checkpoints used to gauge the days work by.

- **First Shot:** This is the first actual filmed shot of the day. It may happen an hour after crew call or three hours after crew call depending on what the first lighting setup is. If it is a big lighting setup, it can take a while to get first shot. An actor may have extensive prosthetics that need to be carefully applied. There might be complications with equipment that can cause delays as well. It can also be delayed by actor's turnaround or any number of things. Regardless of the variables, getting first shot is important. It lets the office and the studio know how the day of shooting is going. In any case, do not forget to call into the production office and let them know when you get your first shot. Producers get very antsy if it is almost lunch and you still have not gotten a first shot. Expect a few tense people if this is the case.

- **Lunch:** Lunch is six hours after general crew call. Unfortunately you will not always break on time. It depends how the shooting day lays out. Be sure to call the Production office when you break for lunch.

   If you do not break on time it's called going into *grace* or *meal penalty violation—MPV* (or invoking the director's grace period). Grace means that if you are in the middle of a scene and it would be disruptive to break for lunch, the director asks the crew for a favor. Grace extends the director's shooting time. If you go past grace, the crew starts to go into meal penalty. Meal penalties differ from show to show. Ask about them before you start shooting. If it is a nonunion show then meal penalties become a producer issue. If you do go into meal penalty, the producers will start to get very tense about this. It means almost everyone working is making overtime. On the set it's known as *ching ching*. If you go over, it's a good idea to let the caterer know, so they can hold off on cooking any more orange roughy or steaks. Also notify the production office know.

- **First Shot After Lunch:** Just like the first shot of the morning. It lets everyone know how long it takes to get rolling after lunch time. If you are picking up where you left off then the lighting might not change; however, if you are into a whole new scene, then it may take a couple of hours.

- **Multiple Locations:** If, in the course of the day, you are at two or three locations, you need to call the Production office. Let them know you are *making the move,* or a *company move*. That way any cast or crew who are en route will know to go to the next location. The company usually forms a big car caravan with one PA who remains at the first location until everyone has packed up and made the move to the second location.

- **Wrap:** The word everyone loves to hear. This means that the unit has finished shooting for the day and everyone is going to pack up and head home. If you are at a *practical location* this could mean a lengthy wrap for the electric department. If you are on a stage or interior it would be what they call a *Hollywood wrap* or a *walkaway*. It's good to know if you are coming back to the same location the next day or if it is a walkaway. This will help you keep the grips and electricians informed, as they usually have the longest wrap out. They can start wrapping some of their cables and equipment in advance.

CALLING THE OFFICE

If you are the keeper of the "set phone" it's a good idea to check in with the Production office periodically. They will give you any important phone messages for the crew and relay any important information. If you are paged, call them back as soon as you can. A billion things will be going on around you, but it's necessary to keep in touch with them. They are your connection to the "real world." If you do not have a set phone, get a roll of quarters to use at a pay phone; or, you can call collect. It's not always easy to find a pay phone. Just do your best. That's all anyone can ask.

THE RINGER

Rule of thumb: Turn the phone off when you have finished your call. The production office can always page you if they need you. There is nothing more embarrassing than having your cellular phone go off on the set in the middle of a take. Not only is it embarrassing but you will be lucky to still be in one piece once the 1st AD and Director have finished chewing you out. I have only seen it happen once in the middle of a tense dialogue scene that the actor was having difficulty with. *Ring. Ring.* I thought the director was going to explode. Luckily, the guilty phone owner owned up (always a good idea), and we moved on to the next shot. Do not let it happen to you. If someone uses your phone, check to see if it is turned off before putting it in your holster. If there are visitors on the set, also re-mind them to turn off their phones (and pagers). It saves everyone a lot of humiliation.

CHARGING THE PHONE

As with radio batteries, do not let the phone die. Keep the charger in the Production trailer and keep the spare charg-ing. When it starts to get low, replace it. You do not want the battery to die when the 1st AD is talking to a producer of the next movie she is going to work on!

WHERE IS THE PHONE?

A commonly asked question when you are the keeper of the set phone. Different crew members will need to use it to call all sorts of people. This is fine. They have needs, too, and calls to make. However, sometimes it is passed around after each person is finished and you could spend a lot of time chasing after it. If you lend your phone, ask the borrower to return it to you when they have finished so the next person in line can use it.

Pager Codes:

911:     Urgent

711:     Semi Urgent

411:     Have
         Information

43770: Hello

18

The Pager

If you are assigned phone duty, usually you will have pager duty as well. The Production office sees the pager as their most reliable way to reach the set. They cannot reach you by phone because the ringers are off, so they page you. Here are a few tips that I found work and save time as well.

VIBRATIONS

Always keep your pager on vibrate. This way you will not wind up embarrassed on the set when your pager beeps loudly.

911

This means "emergency." These three numbers after the phone number mean call back immediately—time is of the essence. Well, that's what it normally means. Unfortunately, it is abused. You may end up not responding because it is not an emergency. I try to talk to the production office when I first start and let them know that I consider 911 either a life and death matter or else an extremely nervous executive back at the studio needs to talk to the director—something along those lines. When you work hand in hand with the Production office it can make your life much easier. Often, they often feel forgotten and unappreciated. If you let them know that their concerns are your concerns, you will have a fabulous team. In order to save time on unnecessary 911s, I use a code.

HAVE A CODE

I use this one when I have too many things to do and not enough time. Since then, I have seen other methods, but find this one works for me. Usually what happens when you are paged is:

- you get paged with the office number
- you call the office back
- they give you a message for the 2nd AD to call the Unit Production Manager
- You hang up and give the message to the 2nd AD.

With a code you save yourself this phone call. With the pager there are a million options. Assign the key crew to a list of numbers and it will save you all a lot of time. The caller then simply inputs the number that corresponds to the person that they need to speak with and it saves a phone call.

1   Director
2   Producer
3   UPM
4   1st AD
5   2nd AD
6   2nd 2nd
7   Camera
8   Electric
9   Grips
10   Hair/Makeup
11   Wardrobe
00   set PA

Now what you can also do is tack a 911 onto the end of the department if it is indeed an urgent matter. A 711 can be used for less urgent messages or 411 if you just need to call in for a bunch of office messages.

Part VI

The Top Ten Reasons
to Work in Production

10. Tasty Food

9. Nice People

8. Travel to Foreign Lands

7. Wear shorts to work
every day

6. See the sunrise and the
sunset at work

5. Learn how to run on four
hours of sleep

4. Get out of Jury Duty

3. You get a Walkie-Talkie

2. Cool Crew Jackets

1. You have a burning
desire to make movies

19

The Production Kit

When you are in pre-production someone in the AD department will prepare the production kit for the set. It usually goes in the production trailer once you start shooting. I have designed my "dream kit." The film budget may not always allow for all these items so review the list with your AD team to see what your budget allows. The kit consists of three elements: forms, filing and supplies.

FORMS

The following forms will be helpful in your kit:
- Time Cards (union and nonunion)
- Extras Vouchers
- Crew Lists
- Contact Lists
- Cast List
- Pager List
- Mobile Phone List
- Room List
- Shooting Schedule
- One Line Schedule
- Day-Out-of-Days
- Maps
- Location List
- Extra's Breakdown
- Crew START Paperwork Packets

- Blank SAG Sheets
- Daily Contracts
- Weekly Contracts
- Accident Reports (blank)
- Workmen's Compensation Forms
- Mileage Forms
- Blank Call Sheets
- Blank Production Reports
- Petty Cash Envelopes
- Petty Cash Forms
- Overnight Delivery/Messenger Service Forms
- Check Requests
- Photo Releases
- 1-9 & W-4 Tax Forms
- Scripts
- Colored Pages (for script revisions)
- Sunrise/Sunset Chart

FILING AND SORTING IT OUT

Create files for the following:
- 1st & 2nd ADs Call Sheets
- Call Sheets
- Production Reports
- Copies of Time Cards
- Safety Memos
- Forms Listed in Part A
- SAG Rules

SUPPLIES

The best office supply organizer I have seen is a fishing tackle box for all the small stuff that needs to be contained.

For the files and the bigger items the Rubbermaid plastic file boxes are great. Here is a suggested list of supplies:

OFFICE SUPPLIES

- A Roll of Quarters
- A Small Paper Cutter (if you have to do the sides on the set)
- Binder Clamps (three different sizes)
- Highlighting Markers
- Hole Punch (one-, two- and three-hole)
- Letter Envelopes
- Little Memo Pads
- Manila Envelopes
- Six Reams of Letter Paper
- Six Reams of Letter Paper (three-hole punch)
- One Case Legal Paper
- One Ream of Blue Legal Paper (for revised call sheets)
- Paper Clips (large and small)
- Pens and Pencils (check with your ADs to see if they prefer a particular kind).
- Red and Black Permanent Markers
- Reinforcements for three-hole punched paper
- Scissors
- Staple Remover
- Stapler and Staples
- Tape and Dispenser (masking, duct/gaffer, regular and double-sided tape)
- Tissues
- White out! All Kinds

MISCELLANEOUS SUPPLIES

- AA Batteries
- AAA Batteries (for pagers)
- Cigarette Lighter
- Flashlight
- Matches
- Safety Pins

FIRST AID AND MEDICAL SUPPLIES

- Adhesive Bandages
- Aspirin
- Cough Drops
- Ibuprofen
- Lip Balm
- Motion Sickness Pills
- Vitamin C

20

Tools

YOUR KIT

Your personal kit is as important as the one you will maintain for the production team. Make sure you find a bag or fanny pack that evenly distributes the weight of everything you need to carry. Some people use a belt for their walkie-talkie. The old Army belts work well as do scuba belts. Whether you carry a fanny pack or not, it's good to have the following things on your person at all times.

- Pens
- Pencils
- Two Call Sheets (one for you and one to give away)
- Mini Notebook
- Mini Crew List
- Mini One-Line Schedule
- Mini Cast List
- Mini Pager List
- Mini Contact List
- White Out
- Mini Flashlight
- Any Personal Items (wallet, keys, tissues, mints, cigarette lighter)

WALKIE-TALKIE WEAR

Your walkie will be attached to your fanny pack or belt. At times it will be cumbersome. Try to switch sides so you distribute the weight you are carrying over time. Although no one has said anything about the ergonomically correct way, it cannot hurt to swap sides. The same goes for the cell phone and pager. I weighed my pack once. It was over 10 lbs. It adds up at the end of the day. You can try a backpack, but in the end the fanny pack has proved to be the most practical. Camera assistants and grips use a waist pack that seems to work well. The walkie belts that most people use can be found at the Army-Navy stores or sporting goods stores. They are durable and wide to help eliminate back pain.

CLIPBOARD

The standard AD or PA clipboard is metal legal size with a hinge on the left side. They are sold at most office supply stores and cost around $30. The outside is a great flat surface for writing notes. Inside, keep the last few days' call sheets and production reports, a schedule and a notebook. You will find, with most of your kit, that everyone has individual needs and you will tailor it to fit your life-style.

PRODUCTION NOTEBOOK

Keep a book with all the phone numbers, schedules and a copy of the script with current revisions. Make sure this travels to the set with you every day, even if you leave it in the back of the car, you have it near you.

GEAR

Depending on where you are shooting will determine what kind of gear you pack. Here is a list that encompasses most weather conditions:

- Comfortable Shoes (running shoes are popular)
- Warm, Waterproof Jacket
- Sweatshirt or Old Sweater
- Extra Socks
- Extra T-shirt
- Hat (one with a brim or visor to protect you from the sun)
- Thermal Underwear
- Gloves
- Sunglasses
- Rain Boots
- Full Rain Gear (you can get the inexpensive kind—unless you are doing a show with lots of rain)
- Sunscreen (look out for your team, too)
- Bandanna (to prevent smoke and dust inhalation. Also good to soak in cold water and wear around your neck in extremely hot weather).
- Heavy Boots or Sorrel's (for extremely cold weather)
- Parka (for extremely cold weather—sometimes this can be inside the sound stage when its 80° outside)
- Hiking Shoes (for more rugged conditions)

STORING AND KEEPING TRACK OF YOUR GEAR

Now stuff everything on the list into a duffel bag! You certainly do not need all this stuff to get started, but as you go from show to show you will want to acquire it. Try to buy the good stuff so it will last. Then you will not have to keep buying it. Also, keep track of the gear you buy. When you return home put it in a plastic bin that says "Location Gear." This way when you are called again to go to New York in the winter, you will have everything ready. Sometimes you will be called to a show and forget you already bought a full Gortex rain suit and buy another one. Keep track of your gear. You will also go through a lot of shoes. You are on your feet constantly, so invest in several pairs of good shoes. Rubber-soled shoes are quiet on the set and easy on your feet.

CATALOG SHOPPING

On location, the cast and crew frequently shop by mail. There is little time on your day off to battle the shops, so catalogs are the perfect solution. Plus they can deliver it straight to the production office. Some of the good catalogs to rely on for quality gear are: J. Crew, LL Bean, North Face, Columbia, Eddie Bauer and Patagonia.

PRODUCTION CLOTHES

You will have production clothes and real-life clothes. Try not to mix them—your production clothes usually end up getting trashed pretty badly.

21

Necessities

FOOD

Make sure that you eat! Arrive at the set early enough to have breakfast. This probably seems so basic but you will get busy and not have time to eat. If you eat first, at least you will have enough energy to get you through the day. Lunch time is about watching the line and catching up on the production report, so try to at least eat breakfast! I know a lot of ADs who wear the martyr hat and will not be seen eating. Yikes! You have to eat to have the energy you need for the rest of the day. Look out for your co-workers too. Offer to bring them a plate of food if they are stuck in a meeting or on the phone.

SHELTER

Your first few jobs on location might be kind of difficult in terms of money. Try to bunk with a few PAs and share the rent so you can stretch your earnings.

DIRTY LAUNDRY

The Production office usually works out a deal with a local laundry to charge you by the pound to wash, fluff and fold your dirty laundry. If you leave your laundry in a bag, and some money in the Production office, your laundry will come back the next day clean and folded. Your day off should be for relaxing, not for doing laundry.

GOOD HEALTH

It is virtually impossible to be sick when you are shooting. Production takes so much energy. You have to stay healthy. Do not expect a lot of sympathy if you are hung over. Follow good habits (healthy food, enough water, etc.) to prevent yourself from getting sick. Try to catch up on sleep on your down days.

TRANSPORTATION

Have a reliable car and *never* come to work late. Get to work at all costs. If your car breaks down, call the production office. Ask them to let the 2nd AD know you will be late on the set. Usually, someone from the transportation department will come and get you or you can take a taxi. Just get to work ASAP. If you have car trouble before you leave your house, let the office know. They can always help you. The "broken down car" routine only works once. Make sure you have plenty of gas and regular tune-ups. If you go on location for a while, give your car a good tune-up upon returning. You have to be at work on time to be effective.

ALARM CLOCK

Get one. In fact, get three. Place them around your room so you will have to get up to turn them off. You will feel horrible if you sleep in and arrive at work late. You do not want the humiliation of getting to work late. There will be plenty of time to sleep when you are waiting for your next job.

THE LOVE CONNECTION

It happens to everyone. Many people fall in love or lust with a co-worker. It happens frequently on location. People work hard and play hard. It happens to even the most disciplined. So, be careful. Location romances are a dime a dozen. If it makes you happy, that's your business. If it affects your career or your *real life*—it's still your business. If you have a fight or break up, it can also make coming to work unbearable.

Part VII

"When I graduated UCLA Film School, I responded to the following ad:

Movie Production Company Seeks Someone Who Can Type, Sew and Drive a Motor Home.
Call 555-1234

I was hired and they had me retype script pages, be a stand-in for an actress, help the Wardrobe Department sew, drive the motor home and lastly I had to dress a hotel room for pickup shots. My advice to PAs: take initiative and do not be afraid to make mistakes."

Marie Cantin, UPM/Line Producer
Dante's Peak, Things To Do In Denver
When You're Dead, Waterdance,
Heart Condition, Somebody To Love

22

Landing Your First Job in Film Production

Congratulations. You are out of school (or almost out) and are ready to work. What do you need to survive in the real world?

1. Experience—Leave college armed with some sort of internship program or work experience. Be willing to pay your dues.
2. Résumé—Your résumé will not be very substantial at first, but as long as you have some work experience under your belt, you will survive.
3. Hit List—A list of the dream companies or people you want to work for.
4. Network and Contacts—Every person who is even remotely connected to the film business has the potential to help you land your first job.
5. Vehicle—Something with two to four wheels that is fairly reliable. You have to be able to transport yourself to and from interviews and, ultimately, work.
6. Map—Know how to maneuver around the city. (Thomas Guide has great maps of the Los Angeles area.)
7. Family and Friends—In the beginning, you may have to lean on these people while you become established.
8. Pager—Be available and ready to start work at any given moment.

9. Perspective—Your big break may not happen right away. Keep an open mind and a positive attitude about your endeavors.
10. Perseverance—A burning, passionate desire to make movies.

WORK EXPERIENCE

There are many ways to acquire your work experience. Here are some routes to gaining that experience:

WORKING FOR COURSE CREDIT

This type of program is usually set up by the college in conjunction with an internship program. It allows a participant to learn from the production experience while receiving credit toward college courses. Hopefully, upon graduation, this will allow you to segue into a full-time paying job with the company. Most colleges will have a file of the companies who accept interns. Take some time to review and research the potential positions.

INTERNSHIPS

Most universities run summer intern programs with the studios in Los Angeles. They try to place you in the type of environment you hope to work in. There may also be internships at your local television station(s), the Academy of Television Arts and Sciences or local production companies. The best way to land an internship is to contact everyone you know in production. Internships are not usually advertised in the newspaper but rather run through the college intern or course for credit programs. Be prepared to do many menial tasks and keep chanting the Golden Rules. It will not be easy—but if you endure—the next paying job that comes up hopefully belongs to you.

MINIMUM WAGE POSITIONS

If you are trying to work on a major motion picture right away, sometimes you will not be allowed to work for free (slavery laws). In this case you may land a job that pays minimum wage. Although you will not get many perks (per diem, travel expenses, etc.) you will be working, earning a credit, and getting experience.

WHY WOULD YOU WANT TO WORK FOR FREE?

Low or no-budget nonunion films need people like you who want to work for free and gain experience. Working for free (or for practically nothing) will help you decide if this is something you want to do. In the production department, you work with all the departments. This gives you a good vantage point to see what department you might grow into. There are many avenues to explore in filmmaking, not only producing and directing.

Working for free also means you stretch out your learning curve. As a production assistant, you can make mistakes. It is beneficial to be in a position where if you do make a mistake it is not a costly one that affects a lot of people. It is a good place to learn from other's mistakes. When the time comes for *you* to make the big decisions you will be a little more experienced. A great deal of crisis management goes on during filmmaking. The more you encounter challenging situations, the more discerning you become and the more equipped you are to handle the *big ones.*

HOW TO MAKE THE MOST OF IT

Be available. Make the most of it. Put on your listening cap. This is not the time to pitch your latest and greatest film idea unless you want to be laughed out of a potentially great opportunity. One of the best things about being an intern is that you will do many small tasks that will not make sense at all. However, if you *are* paying attention, you will start acquiring a sense of the "Big Picture" and how everything fits together. Another asset is the people you are meeting. These are the first of many contacts you will meet in the industry.

PAYING YOUR DUES

Working for little or no money is inconceivable to some people. However, sometimes it's about paying your dues. It's about proving that you want to be in production and that you, too, have done many menial jobs in exchange for being able to learn from the true pros. It is not unusual to find highly educated people working as assistants. It is very clear when someone on the set has not paid their dues. Paying your dues teaches you about respect and helps you understand that everyone's job is important and integral to creating the end product. If you make a decision to be in production, you should commit to working with little or no pay for one or two jobs. It will be difficult, but the reward comes under a big category called "experience." Soon the money will start rolling in *and* you will be paid overtime to boot.

HOW DO I GET A JOB WORKING FOR FREE?

Put yourself out there. Pound the streets, visit your friends who work at studios and production companies, knock on doors, and make phone calls. Some people might think you are a little crazy to work for free—but if you do a good job for them, you will be high on their list when a paying job becomes available.

Here's a sample phone call:

> YOU
> "Hi! Do you have any projects coming up?"

> PRODUCTION OFFICE
> "Yes."

> YOU
> "I'd love to work for you."

> PRODUCTION OFFICE
> "What can you do?"

> YOU
> "Anything to do with film or TV production."

> PRODUCTION OFFICE
> Are you a student?"

> YOU
> "I am."

> PRODUCTION OFFICE
> "Can you make coffee?"

> YOU
> "YES!" *(Rule #1)*

> PRODUCTION OFFICE
> "Good Coffee?"

> YOU
> "I make great coffee."

> PRODUCTION OFFICE
> "Can you make copies?"

```
                    YOU
    "Sure I know how to run a
    copier."

                    PRODUCTION OFFICE
    "Do you file?"

                    YOU
    "Sure I know how to file."

                    PRODUCTION OFFICE
    "Why do you want to do this?"

                    YOU
    "I just want to work in produc-
    tion."

                    PRODUCTION OFFICE
    "All right, when can you start?"

                    YOU
    "I'm available right now."

                    PRODUCTION OFFICE
    "I'll call you a drive-on."
```

If you live in Los Angeles (LA) there are opportunities everywhere you look. Schools and start-up production companies need people who want to break in. Short films and low-budget features happen every day in LA. If you do not live in LA, do your homework. Call all the production companies. Find out what films or TV shows are coming to town so you can work as a "local." Talk to your local film commission (listed in the phone book) and ask them about the projects that will shoot in your area.

Regardless of where you live, talk to everyone you know who works in production. Take anything that they will give you. Do you know how many "pros" started out answering phones, serving coffee, pounding nails or watering plants? No matter what you end up doing, you will learn something. The more you learn, the more you know. The more you know, the more prepared you are to make a decision about where you fit in. Once you find out where you fit in, you can make your plan to get there.

HAVE A PLAN

Take a few moments to sit down and analyze what you want. Write down a plan for your first couple of years out of school (boot camp) and then a five year plan and perhaps a longer term plan. Your plans may change, but at least you will have one in place if for some reason you forget where you are headed. Try to be realistic.

YOUR RÉSUMÉ

Your résumé is your calling card. Hopefully, it will get you an interview. Keep it simple and short—one page and possibly a second page for references. Make sure the information is accurate; do not embellish. List your phone number and pager number clearly. Make sure there are no typos. Use a font that is clear and easy to read. Do not worry about fancy paper. Have a stack of current résumés standing by. Drop your résumé off in person if it is an option. It is a good way for the potential employer to put your name with a face. Write a simple cover letter. Do not tell your life story. Do not tell them how many times you have watched their movies. Let your résumé speak for itself.

Then follow up with a phone call once you send your résumé out to your "hit list."

THE HIT LIST

Make a list of the people you want to learn from. If you get an interview, do your homework and make sure you know something about the company and the person who is interviewing you. Read the trades and industry magazines. Treat your job hunt as a giant research project. Dream big. What have you got to lose?

Networking and Contacts

MAKING CONTACTS

Do not be shy. Everyone you meet, in Hollywood anyway, is somehow related to this industry. Some will be more willing to help you than others; you will sort those out on your own. At first you will only know a handful of people, but that handful knows another handful of people and so on, and so on.

TRACKING YOUR HIT LIST

Keep a list of everyone who received your résumé. Make a note once you place your follow up call. Make a note if they send you a letter stating that they are not hiring at this time. Note any special information about the company. Make a note of the assistant's name or any other particulars. If your job search is taking longer than you had anticipated, refresh your hit list. Perhaps it was too narrow to begin with.

KEEPING YOUR CONTACTS

Now that you have met a handful of wonderful people, make sure you do not lose them. Many people started out like you and they will want to help you along. Hold onto those people and nurture the relationships. It is an investment you will never regret. A phone call is fine to check in. Keep it short. Time is money. Occasionally, it's nice to send something in the mail: an updated résumé, an article that relates to them, a birthday card, or a postcard from location. Ultimately, it's a relationship and it takes work and communication to keep it alive.

WHEELS

Have a vehicle that can get you from interview to interview. In Los Angeles you are at a definite disadvantage without wheels. In New York you may get by taking taxis, as they are readily available.

MAPS

The Thomas Bros. Guide or a quality map of the city will help you find your way to interviews. It will become very helpful once you are hired and are traveling to location every day.

FAMILY AND FRIENDS

Many times your family or close friends can help you with room and board until you are making enough money to live on your own. In the beginning the cash may be a little slim as you get your experience badge. It helps to have the support of friends and family as you begin your big adventure. If your family is unable to help, find a way to make it.

PAGER

If you can afford a pager, it's a great thing to have. It will mean that you can be reached at any given moment for an interview or for work. They are not that expensive any more. If you can afford it, get one.

PERSPECTIVE

Keep your eye on the goal. Keep reviewing your hit list. Try to stay positive and focused on what you desire. Do not feel sorry for yourself! If it does not happen like you thought it would, perhaps there is a reason. Keep your sense of humor and an open mind.

PERSEVERANCE

If you want it and are working hard at it, something will give way. Try not to be discouraged. You have to want it. Unfortunately, there are many other people who also want what you want. You have to want it more. The good news is: there are plenty of jobs and plenty of movies to make. Go for it!

23

Future Jobs

CAREER OPTIONS

There are many options as you start to gain solid experience on the set. Here are some ideas that may work for you. Whatever you do, follow your passion.

WHERE CAN YOU GO FROM HERE

You can go anywhere you want to. By now you have started to get a solid core of set experience. Maybe it is for you and maybe it's not. Once you have mastered the art of being a set PA you will start to feel as if there is something more. Perhaps you have learned everything there is to learn or perhaps there is a job that you have your eye on, since you have been in a good vantage point to see everything. Perhaps you have decided to be an assistant director. Whatever it is, know when it is time to move up or move on. It is unbearable to be around people who are no longer happy with what they are doing. There are lots of options and by now you will have a long list of contacts and resources to put your plan into action. In order to grow, you need to stretch. No one was ever successful taking the easy route. Here are some typical progressions:

FROM PA TO 2ND 2ND AD

This jump takes the longest because it requires getting into the *Directors Guild of America (DGA)*. Once you are in the DGA, you are ready to begin your ascent toward being a 1st AD. If you work consistently and enter the DGA by saving your days, it will take you anywhere from two to five years of being a set PA before you get in the DGA. The time is shortened to two years if you are accepted into the Directors Guild's Assistant Directors Training Program.

FROM 2ND 2ND TO 2ND AD

This should take about two to four years. The jobs are entirely different. It may happen sooner than I have estimated. It depends when you are ready. It gets more difficult as you climb. Once you are in the DGA, the money gets much better. It's hard to accept the idea that you might have to turn down a few job offers—hoping that a 2nd AD gig will come along.

FROM 2ND AD TO 1ST AD

This is the giant step as far as your career development is concerned. If you have come this far you have demonstrated your ability to command a set. It's a huge commitment. It is also the reason that some good 2nd ADs who would be great 1st ADs, never make the jump. Being a 1st is a completely different type of responsibility. Some 2nd ADs do not want the added stress. This jump can take from two to six years. Hopefully you can surround yourself with people who believe in you and, so, your transition will move swiftly.

FROM PA TO ETERNITY

Your options are endless. If you decide you do not want to be an AD but you still want to work in film or television production, this is no problem at all. If you have done eight to ten shows as a set PA and are equipped with some of the positive habits in this book, then you will probably be a welcome addition to any department. They already know you work hard and are not afraid to put in long hours and have a working knowledge of set operations. They can count on you to get the job done. You can be an assistant to a producer or director, or change tracks and go to work at an agency and learn about the other side of Hollywood. (Read Hugh Taylor's book, *The Hollywood Job Hunters Survival Guide* for a good discussion of this.) There are many choices and opportunities—do not get discouraged.

Documentation

The following is a list of the paperwork you should hold onto from each show. You will need these when it comes time to qualify for the DGA. Documentation is important.

CALL SHEETS

Organize these by show in chronological order. Make sure if you do work, that your name is on the call sheet. If it's not, it will be hard to prove that you worked on that show.

PRODUCTION REPORTS

Organize these by show in chronological order. Again, your name should be on the production report to prove your work history.

DEAL MEMO

Whatever contract, formal or informal, that you signed that outlines your deal points.

PAY STUBS

Organize these by show in chronological order. These will also be required by the DGA when you are trying to qualify.

CREW LISTS

This is another way of validating your employment with a show. I like to keep a separate book with all of my past crew lists. It will help you when you are looking for quality crew people and to keep in touch with all the good contacts you are nurturing. Organize them chronologically in a three-ring binder by show.

Phone Calls and Follow-Up

CHECKING IN

In order to maintain your contacts, you will need to check in with them every so often. A quick phone call or postcard will remind them that you are still in the thick of things and working hard. I usually go right through my crew list book and call everyone I would like to work with again.

SAMPLE CONVERSATION

```
              YOU
   Hi.  It's April.  Got a minute?
              PRODUCTION OFFICE
   Yes.  Just a minute.
              YOU
   I'm checking in.
```

```
          PRODUCTION OFFICE
Okay.

               YOU
I wanted to let you know I am
available in May when OUT COLD
wraps.
          PRODUCTION OFFICE
Great, good to know.

               YOU
How are you?
          PRODUCTION OFFICE
Good. Swamped.

               YOU
Okay. I'll talk to you soon.
Bye-bye.
```

Like that. Short and simple. Do not waste their time.

RETURNING CALLS

If someone calls you, try to call them back on the same day. People will call you to work even though you may be on a job. Call them back that day. Let them know you are flattered that they thought of you. Unfortunately, you are working, but you hope you will have the opportunity to work with them in the future. Even if they are not calling about work, try to return the call that day. It's a good habit.

YOUR RÉSUMÉ

Keep it short! Keep it current. In the beginning you will not have very many shows, so it is all right to include a lot of the extraneous things that everyone puts down as filler. As you work more and add credits to your resume, streamline it. A good résumé is still one page, two tops. Include the show, the studio (if it was a studio show, or the independent production company name), the name and title of the show's producer, the name and title of the person(s) you worked for. That's it. Dates are okay if you need filler. They also show a progression. One or two pages—that's it. [A tip: When you first start out and you want your résumé to look substantial even though there isn't much on it, increase the font size to 14 point.] As you work more decrease it to keep it all to one page. I would not go much smaller than 10 point. It gets a little hard to read.

If someone asks for your résumé, try to fax it to them that day. This is why you should always keep it up to date and keep some copies with you in your clipboard. You are ready and you want it.

FOLLOW-UP

When you are job-hunting *follow-up* is very important. If you send your résumé, call to make sure it gets into the right hands. Wait a day then call to follow-up. Films sometimes start and finish in the course of a day. You could send your résumé to a show that ends up getting pushed or canceled entirely. For this reason, do not be pesky but keep on top of the progress of the show. Keep looking until you have a solid job offer.

PA KARMA

What goes around comes around. This is an abundant universe with plenty of films and opportunities. If you are lucky enough to be working and you get a call to do another job, do not quit your job! Do not quit a gig unless it is totally unbearable or it is violating your code. If you are working and you get a call, pass the job along to someone else who is looking. Maybe someday you will need work and that job will come back to you. Do good work and it will come back to you.

"I was working at Universal in television as a clerical assistant and was accepted into the very first Assistant Director Training Program. The day before I started the program a junior executive in the film department called me upstairs to give me a few tips about being a production assistant. He said:
1. Never Sit Down.
2. Always wear a tie on the set.
3. Do not do your paperwork on the set.
The project was called *Voyage To The Bottom Of The Sea*. The first day I was there I stood all day wearing a tie and no one gave me anything to do. I think they thought I was a studio spy. The training program was brand new and no one knew what to do with me. After about five days of standing, they let me do a call sheet.
As far as advice for PAs today—be aggressive in a positive way. Find a way to be assertive without being pushy. I actually saw a PA sleeping today with their walkie-talkie blaring loudly. I know they work hard, but I am not that impressed with sleeping on the job. Be involved. Be present."

Art Levinson
Unit Production Manager/Line Producer
The Flood, Great Balls Of Fire, Little Nikita, Mr. Mom,
My Favorite Year, Shampoo (1st Ad),
All The President's Men (1st Ad)

24

The DGA

WHAT IS IT?

The Director's Guild of America (DGA) was established in 1936 by 12 feature film directors, in order to provide proper recognition and creative freedom for all directors. It was designed to protect the director and his or her *creative rights.* The DGA currently has more than 10,000 members whose work is represented in theater, feature films, educational, industrial and documentary films, as well as television (live and taped), radio, videos and commercials. The guild includes: directors, line producers, unit production managers, 1st assistant directors, 2nd assistant directors, associate directors, production associates, and stage managers (on the East Coast, location managers are also DGA members). Although it will be a very long walk to make it into the DGA, it is well worth it if you plan on being in the business awhile. It is designed to protect you creatively, but it also has great health insurance and benefits.

HOW TO GET IN

There are a few avenues into the guild as you climb the ranks as a set PA. As you move closer to "getting all of your days," keep in touch with the *DGA Contract Adminis-tration* so you do not miss any steps. For most membership routes it is essential to save the following documents to qualify: deal memos, pay stubs, call sheets, production reports and crew lists. Save these documents by production in chronological order. If your documentation is not assembled in order, it will not even be reviewed. It is also suggested that you make copies of everything you send and keep the originals for yourself.

Listed below are some of the major avenues for qualification. Check with the East and/or West Coast DGA Contract Administration office for changes to policies and procedures.

SOUTHERN CALIFORNIA BASIC OR QUALIFICATION LIST

Southern California is defined as the area between San Luis Obispo and the California–Mexico border. Work for 400 days as a 2nd AD, 1st AD or UPM in the production of motion pictures. Of the 400 days, no more than 25% can be spent in prep and 75% must be spent with the actual shooting company.

THIRD AREA BASIC LIST

Third Area is defined as everywhere except Southern California and New York. Work for 120 days as a 2nd AD, 1st AD or UPM in the production of motion pictures. Of the 120 day, no more than 25% can be spent in prep and 75% must be spent shooting.

THE EASTERN OR WESTERN REGION COMMERCIAL LIST

If you work 600 set PA days on the East Coast you can be added to the Commercial qualification list that allows you to work as a 2nd AD on commercials, everywhere BUT Los Angeles. With an additional 150 days as a commercial 2nd AD you can upgrade to a commercial 1st AD. As a commercial 1st AD you are eligible to transfer to the Southern California list as a Feature 2nd AD.

GETTING GRANDFATHERED IN

This does not happen often so it's best not to bank on it. Getting "grandfathered" into the DGA means that you were working on a nonunion show (usually outside LA on location) and then the show turned union. If they are unable to come up with a 2nd AD in the area, then you can get grandfathered in. Like everything, this event can swing one of two ways. If you are grandfathered in and you have been a hard working PA saving your days with a good five shows under your belt, it's great. You deserve to move up early. However, if it is your first or second show and it happens, be careful. At first it may look like you hit the motherload, but think about it. You are going to have no experience and everyone is going to make you aware of this. You also may run into a shortage of days or be limited to working only Third Area for a while. Hopefully you will have a solid base of contacts to draw on to keep working. I am not saying do not take it if it is offered. However, be aware of some of the potential consequences and start doing some major homework.

THE DGA ASSISTANT DIRECTORS TRAINING PROGRAM

The training program was established in 1965 by the Directors Guild of America and the Alliance of Motion Picture and Television Producers. The program's main purpose is to train 2nd ADs for the motion picture and television industry.

The program will put you through 400 days of on-the-set training as well as regular seminars. It emphasizes administrative, managerial and interpersonal skills. To apply for the program you must be 21 years of age, have a Bachelor's or Associates Degree or 520 days of paid work in film or television production. College credits, military service (E-5 or above) and work experience may be combined to meet the eligibility requirements. The program is highly competitive. Of the 2,000—4,000 applicants they get every year only 700 are accepted to take the test. After the test a smaller group of under 120 is selected to an interview and assessment. Of the 100, between 25-50 are selected each year. It is a quality program that teaches you the nuts and bolts of being an assistant director.

NEW YORK DGA TRAINING PROGRAM

The New York program has looser requirements than the West Coast program. They still require a certain amount of days but you do not have to have your college degree. Check with the New York DGA Training Program for specifics.

DGA Contact Information

WEST COAST OFFICE

The Directors Guild of America
7920 Sunset Boulevard
Los Angeles, CA 90046
Phone: 310-289-2000
Fax: 310-289-2029

MIDWEST OFFICE

The Directors Guild of America
400 North Michigan Avenue, Suite 307
Chicago, IL 60611
Phone: 312-644-5050
Fax: 312-644-5776

EAST COAST OFFICE

The Directors Guild of America
110 West 57th Street
New York, NY 10019
Phone: 212-581-0370
Fax: 212-581-1441

DGA Qualification and Assistant Directors Training Program

DGA CONTRACT ADMINISTRATION

15503 Ventura Boulevard
Encino, CA 91436-3103
Contact: Maureen Fleming
Phone: 818-382-1741

ASSISTANT DIRECTORS TRAINING PROGRAM

15503 Ventura Boulevard

Encino, CA 91436-3103

Contact: Elizabeth Stanley

Phone: 818-386-2545

Website: http://dga.org/trainingprogram

DGA Membership

DGA MEMBERSHIP

7920 Sunset Boulevard

Los Angeles, CA 90046

Contact: Kathleen Newman

Phone: 310-289-2077

Fax: 310-289-2029

Send DGA Application to:

Maureen Fleming

DGA Contract Administration

15503 Ventura Boulevard

Encino, CA 91436-3103

Third Area or Commercial Qualification List

THIRD AREA BASIC OR
SOUTHERN CALIFORNIA BASIC LIST

15503 Ventura Boulevard

Encino, CA 91436-3103

Contact: Maureen Fleming

Phone: 818-382-1741

THIRD AREA OR BASIC QUALIFICATION LIST

1697 Broadway
New York, NY 10019
Contact: Sandra Forman
Phone: 212-397-0930
Fax: 212-664-1626

EASTERN AND WESTERN REGION COMMERCIAL LIST

1697 Broadway
New York, NY 10019
Contact: Sandra Forman
Phone: 212-397-0930
Fax: 212-664-1626

NEW YORK AREA QUALIFICATION LIST

(Under the DGA Basic Agreement)
Contact: Janice Scambino
914-747-2979

Send DGA Application to:

Maureen Fleming
DGA Contract Administration
15503 Ventura Boulevard
Encino, CA 91436-3103

Forms

Exec. Producer:
Producer:
Co-Producer:

Director:
FITZSIMMONS

TEST DRIVE

CALL TIME: 0730 A
SHOOTING CALL: 0830 A
DAY:
OUT OF: 3 OF 40
Low
High 70° Sunny
SAFETY MEETING @ CALL

Nearest Hospital: CEDARS
Beach Water Temp: N/A

WEDNESDAY
April 2, 1997

SCENES	SET	CAST NO.	D/N	PAGES	LOCATION
Sc. 7	EXT. OPEN ROAD		DAY		ROAD X
Sc. 7B	MAGGIE + VICTOR FIGHT				PLLLHS TOWN
Sc. 11	AS BEN TRIES TO				TEXAS
Sc. 13	FIX CAR.				

No.	CAST	PART OF	MAKE-UP	ON SET	STATUS	REMARKS
1	C. JANE	MAGGIE	0700	0730		
2	S. UPTON	VICTOR	0700	0730		
3	H. RICHARD	BEN				

Special Additives

DUST-FX   WETDOWN-FX
HERO CAR   WARDROBE : DIRTY   CRANE

ADVANCE SCHEDULE

SCENES	SET	CAST NO.	D/N	LOCATION
13	EXT. OPEN ROAD			
22				
19	INT. CAR - THEY FIGHT			INSERT CAR

DUST   CRANE
WIND   WETDOWN
INSERT CAR

1st AD: 2nd AD: Set Phone:
** NO FORCED CALLS WITHOUT PRIOR APPROVAL OF UPM. **

	INT CAPTAIN'S QUARTERS		Night	TBD	
136pt	Capt Everton tries again to kill himself	3	Day	Stage 6	
	INT COMMUNICATIONS ROOM				
207pt	Capt Alexi scolds Nadia	6, 13	Day	Stage 8	
	INT VOLKOV MISSILE ROOM				
	Goliath is hit with rubber hose				

MONDAY April Fool's Day, 1997 SHOOT DAY 34

Call Sheet (Front)

TEST DRIVE

	Position	Name	TIME
		PRODUCTION	
1	Director	FITZSIMMONS, A.	0630
1	Prod. Mgr.	DOWNER, J.	o/c
1	1st Asst. Director	ORNSTEIN, D.	0630
1	Key 2nd Asst. Dir.	MURPHY, M.	
1	Key Set PA	JEFFERSON, M.	
1	Set PA	GUTHRIE, J	
1	Set PA		

		PRODUCTION OFFICE	
1	Prod. Secretary	CAMPOS, C.	o/c
1	Office PA		

		CAMERA	
1	Director of Photog.	GARDEN, D	0630
1	Camera Operator	PER D.G.	0700
1	1st Asst. Camera		
1	2nd Asst. Camera		
1	1st Asst. Camera		
1	Loader		

		SCRIPT	
1	Script Supervisor	HORGAN, D.	0630

		VISUAL EFFECTS	
	Visual Effects Consult.	N/A	0700

		VIDEO ASSIST	
1	Video Assist Op	SMITH, A.	0700

		ELECTRIC	
1	Gaffer	LIGHTFOOT, D.	0700
1	Best Boy		
1	Electrician		
1	Electrician		
1	Electrician		

		GRIP	
1	Key Grip	STRONG, I.	0700
1	Best Boy		
1	Dolly Grip		
1	Add'l Grip		
1	Add'l Grip		

Call Sheet (Back)

TEST DRIVE

CALL TIME: 7:30 A.M.

#	Position	Name	TIME
		MAKEUP/HAIR	
1	Hair	JUAN, M.	
1	Make Up	KASTNER DELAGO	0700
		PROP DEPARTMENT	
1	Property Master	CENICEROS, J.C.	0700
1	On Set Dresser		
		WARDOBE	
1	Costumer	NUSSEN DEN, I	0700
		CATERING	
	Breakfast 90		
	Lunch ready @	1:30 P.M.	
		TRANSPORTATION	
1	Driver	CARR, J.	0630
		CRAFT SERVICE	
1	Craft Service	CALOREE, J	0630
1	Set Medic	NANCY, N	0630
		SPFX	
1	FX Coordinator	BLOW IT, F.	0700
1	FX worker		
1	FX worker		
		SOUND	
1	Mixer	MEAGHER, J	0700
		VIDEO	
1			

Call Sheet (Back)

WRAP REPORT

Title: TEST DRIVE   Day #: 3   Date: 3-7-97

Crew Call: 7³⁰A   Shooting Call: 8³⁰A   1st Shot: 8³⁹A

Lunch: 1³⁰P til 2P   1st Shot After Lunch: 3P

Other: — til —   1st Shot After Other: —

	Scenes	Pages		Minutes	Set-ups	Added Scenes	Retaken Pages	Retaken Scenes
Script	168	101	Previous	6:00	37	—	—	—
Previous	4	6	Today	2:00	17	—	—	—
Today	4	2⅛	Total	8:00	54	—	—	—
Total	8	8⅛						
To Do	160	92⅞						

Scene Nos: 7, 7B, 11, 13p+   Added Scenes: —

Scenes Sched. but not shot: N/A   Omitted Scenes: —

CAMERA WRAP: 7P   Retakes: —

Days Work Complete? (YES)/ NO

Comments:

ACAM, BCAM, STEADICAM

Script Supervision: S·N· ZIPP

TEST DRIVE

FEATURE DAILY
PRODUCTION REPORT

Day/Date: 3-7-97	1ST UNIT	Day # 3 of 40

Exec. Producer: V. Flooger Producer: L. Tateeshi Co-Producer:
Prod. No. 37373

Director: A. Fitzsimmons
Weather: Sunny 70°

STATUS OF SHOOTING

	1ST UNIT	2ND UNIT	TEST	REHEARSE	TRAVEL	HOLIDAYS	TURN-AROUND	RETAKES/ADD. SCS.	TOTAL
NO. DAYS SCHEDULED	40	10	1	5	2	—	—		58
NO. DAYS ACTUAL	3	2	1	5	1	—	—		12

DATE STARTED: 3-5-97
SCHEDULED FINISH: 4-9-97
EST. FINISH:

NAME OF SET	LOCATION	SCENE #'S
EXT. OPEN ROAD	DUMSTOWN, TX	7, 7B, 11, 13pt

☑ ON SCHEDULE
☐ AHEAD ___ DAYS
☐ BEHIND ___ DAYS

CREW CALL 7:30A
SHOOTING CALL 8:30A

	SCENES	PAGES		MINUTES	SET-UPS	SCENES COMPLETED:
SCRIPT	168	101		6:00	37	7, 7B, 11, 13pt
OMITS	—	—	PREV.			
TAKEN PREV.	4	6		2:00	17	* SCENES NOT COMPLETE:
TAKEN TODAY	4	2⅛	TODAY			—
TOTAL TO DATE	8	8⅛		8:00	54	
TO BE TAKEN	160	92⅞	TOTAL			

FIRST SHOT 8:30A
MEAL OUT 1:00P
MEAL IN 2P
FIRST SHOT 3P
MEAL OUT —
MEAL IN —

SPECIAL NOTES: A CAM, B CAM, STEADICAM

SOUND	
PREVIOUS	2
TODAY	2
TOTAL	4
WILDTRACK	—

CAM WRAP 7P
CREW WRAP 7P
LAST MAN OUT: 8P
LAST ARRIVAL @ H.Q. —

FILM USE

5248	Print	No Good	Waste	Short Ends	Total	5298	Print	No Good	Waste	Short Ends	TOTAL
Previous	8550	500	—	100	9150	Previous	—	—	—	—	—
Today	4000	150	—	50	4200	Today	—	—	—	—	—
To Date	12550	650	—	150	13350	To Date	—	—	—	—	—

	Print	No Good	Waste	Short Ends	Total	Inventory	5293	5298	5248	TOTAL
Previous	—	—	—	—	—	Starting	—	20,000	50,000	70,000
Today	—	—	—	—	—	Rec'd. Today	—	—	5,000	5,000
To Date	—	—	—	—	—	Used Today	—	—	13350	13350
						On Hand	—	20,000	41650	61650

CAST - WEEKLY AND DAY PLAYERS

CAST	CHARACTER	W/H/S/R/T/D/M	M-UP W/DBL.	REPORT ON SET	DISMISS ON SET	OUT	IN	LEAVE FOR LOC.	ARRIVE ON LOC.	LEAVE LOC.	ARRIVE AT HDG.	STUNT ADJ.	M/P/V
C. Jane	MAGGIE	✓	W	7A	8A	7P	12	2P	650A	7A	7P	710P	—	—
S. Upton	VICTOR	✓	W	7A	8A	7P	12	2P	650A	7A	7P	710P	—	—
M. Ricardo	BEN	✓	W	7A	8A	7P	1	2P	650A	7A	7P	710P	—	—

ALL SAG OUT TIMES INCL. CONTRACTUAL 15 MINUTE CLEANUP

EXTRAS/STAND-INS	NO.	RATE	CALL	DISMISS	MEAL	MPV	ADJ.	NO.	RATE	CALL	DISMISS	MEAL	MPV	ADJ.
	3	100	7A	7P	½	—	—							

ASSISTANT DIRECTORS:

CO-PRODUCER/UPM:
UNIT PRODUCTION MANAGERS:

Production Report (Front)

PRODUCTION REPORT DATE: 3-7-97

POSITION	NAME	IN	OUT
PRODUCTION - SET			
1 U.P.M.	J. BILMER	6.5	20.0
1 U.P.M.			
1 1st Asst. Dir.	J. BILMER	6.5	20.0
1 2nd Asst. Dir.	P. Johnson	6.5	20.5
1 2nd 2nd Asst. Dir.	A. Henrig	6.5	20.5
1 Key Set P.A.	D. Cole		
1 Set P.A.	B. Forten	↓	↓
1 Add'l P.A.			
Asst. to:			
1 Asst. to			
1 Asst. to			
1 Script Supervisor	D. Harptrree	7.0	19.6
CAMERA			
1 Director of Photography	D. GARDEN	7.0	19.5
1 Camera Operator	C. SILK		
1 1st Assistant Camera	J. LIMBO		
1 2nd Assistant Camera			
1 Loader			
1 B Camera Operator			
1 B Camera 1st Assistant			
1 B Camera 2nd Assistant			
1 Still Photographer	S. HUTBUG	7.0	19.0
SHOCKWAVE			
1 Shockwave			
1 Playback Supervisor			
2 Asst. Playback Operator			
GRIP			
1 Key Grip	J. RIGGER	7.0	19.6
1 Best Boy Grip		7.5	19.5
1 Dolly Grip	Per J Rigger		
1 Grip			
1 Grip			
1 Grip			
1 Grip			
1 Add'l. Grip(s)			
1 Key Rigging Grip			
1 Best Boy Rig. Grip			
Rigging Grip (s)			
ELECTRICAL			
1 Gaffer	L. LUCKLIGHT	7.0	19.5
1 Best Boy Electric	J. JUICE	7.5	19.5
1 On-Set Best Boy			
1 Electrician	Per J. Juice		
1 Electrician			
1 Electrician			
1 Dimmer Board Operator			
Add'l. Electrician(s)			
1 Rigging Gaffer			
1 Rigging Best Boy			
2 Rigging Electric			
2 Rigging Electric			
PROPERTY			
1 Property Master	S. DUSTBALL	7.5	19.5
1 Asst. Prop Master	E. CHICKORY	7.5	19.5
1 2nd Asst. Props			
1 Asst. Props			
SOUND/VIDEO			
1 Sound Mixer	S. CANHEAR	7.5	19.5
1 Boom Operator	M. LONGSTICK	7.5	19.5
1 Cableperson	J. CHASE	7.5	19.5
1 Video Assist			
SPECIAL MECHANICAL EFFECTS			
1 SPFX Coordinator	N/A	N/A	N/A
1 Gen. Foreman (machine shop)			
1 Gen. Foreman			
1 Gen. Foreman			
1 Foreman			
1 SPFX TECHS			
1 Robotic Mechanical Super.			
1 Robotic Foreman	N/A	N/A	N/A
1 Body			
1 Painter Model			
1 Model Legs			
1 Mech B Stop			
1 All FX Techs			
1 Cables			
1 Computers			
1 Cosmetic Hands			
1 Mech Cables			
1 Computer			
1 Computer			
1 Robotics & Prosthetics			
1 Bio-Mech Super	N/A	N/A	N/A
1 Bio-Mech 1st Asst.			
1 Droid Super			
1 Bio-Mech Asst.			
1 Droid Asst.			
1 Robotic Asst.			
SPECIAL VFX			
1 VFX Producer	N/A		
1 VFX Coordinator			
1 VFX Project Mgr.			
1 VFX Production Coord.			
MARINE DEPARTMENT			
1 Marine Coordinator			
1 Marine Project Mgr.	N/A	N/A	N/A
1 Marine Foreman			
1 Marine Electrician			
1 Boat/Diver			
2 Boat Crew/Welder			
2 Boat Crew/Welder			
2 Boat Crew			
2 Tug SFX			
MISC. NOTES			
• SAFETY MEETING HELD AT			
	0800 in Catering		

POSITION	NAME	IN	OUT
WARDROBE			
1 Costume Supervisor	N. Hanger	6.5	20.0
1 Key Costumer	S. Soisers	↓	↓
1 Costumer	S. Needles	↓	↓
1 Dresser			
1 Add'l. Costumer(s)			
MAKE-UP & HAIR			
1 Key Make-Up Artist	J. DONUT	7.0	19.5
1 Asst. Make-up Artist	L. CLIPS	↓	↓
1 Make-up Artist	A. SPRAY	↓	↓
1 Key Hairstylist			
1 Asst. Hairstylist			
EXTRAS CASTING			
1 Extra's Casting Director			
ART DEPT.			
1 Production Designer	S. ASVETE	O/C	O/C
1 Art Director	R. ALLBRIGHT		
1 Asst. Art Director	J. FORTNITE	↓	↓
1 Art Dept. Coordinator			
1 Set Designer			
1 Storyboard Artist			
1 Art Asst.(VA)			
SET DECORATING			
1 Set Decorator	J. LOVELACE	O/C	O/C
1 Leadman			
1 Leadman			
1 Buyer/Set Dresser			
1 Set Dressers			
1 Set Dressers/Electric			
1 Set Dec. P.A.			
1 On-Set Dresser			
1 Stby Painter			
CONSTRUCTION			
1 Construction Coord.			
1 Construction Coord.- VA			
1 General Foreman			
1 Labor Foreman			
1 Foreman			
1 Gang Boss			
1 Const. Buyer/Auditor			
1 Stby Carpenter			
PRODUCTION - OFFICE			
1 Production Coordinator	C. CAMFOGS	O/C	O/C
1 Asst. POC	J. DORIGHT		
1 Asst. POC-LA	A. NOTSO	↓	↓
1 Asst. POC			
1 Production Secretary			
1 Office P.A.			
1 Office P.A.			
1 Office P.A.-LA			
LOCATIONS			
1 Location Manager	R. FINDER	O/C	O/C
1 Locations Assistant			
ACCOUNTING			
1 Accountant	J. BEENCNTR	O/C	O/C
1 1st Assistant Accountant	T. MONEYBAG		
2 2nd Asst./Payroll Acct.			
2 2nd Asst./Payroll Acct.			
CRAFT SERVICE			
1 Craft Service			
1 Asst. Craft Service			
CATERER	CHRIS ROSEBUD		
1 Breakfasts	Total # 90		
1 Lunches	Total # 90		
SAFETY & SECURITY			
1 First Aid	PER PROD	↓	↓
1 EMS/Ambulance			
1 Security	↓		
1 Police	↓		
1 Firemen	↓		
EDITORIAL			
1 Editor	J. CUTS	O/C	O/C
1 1st Assistant Editor	S. SLIP		
1 2nd Assistant Editor	R. PASTE	↓	↓
1 Editing P.A.			
PUBLICITY			
1 Story and Associates			
TRANSPORTATION			
1 Transportation Coord.	J. CARDS	O/C	O/C
1 Transportation Captain	PER J. CARDS		
1 Transportation Co-Captain			
1 Transportation Assts.			
1 Drivers			
1 Special Equipment/Driver			
1 Driver Assistant			
1 Camera Trailer			
1 Sound Truck			
1 Grip Truck			
1 Elec. Truck			
1 Prop Truck			
1 SPFX Truck			
1 Make-up Trailer			
1 Wardrobe Trailer			
1 Fuel Truck			
1 Cast Cars	WINDRED/TAYLOR/LANIER	PER RS	
1 Stake beds			
EQUIPMENT			
1 Cameras	ARRI, BEAM SCAM	3	
1 Walkies	60 SINGLE	60	
1 60' Condor			
1 35' Condors			
1 Giraffe Crane			
1 Hybrid			
1 Pee Wee Dolly	DOLLY		
ADD'L. EQUIPMENT			
ADD'L NOTES:	NO MPU'S		

Production Report (Back)

SCREEN ACTORS
PRODUCTION TIME REPORT

DATE: 3-7-97

PAGE 1 OF 1

PICTURE TITLE: TEST DRIVE

PRODUCTION CO.: TEST DRIVE FILM CO.
PROD. NO: 37373
CONTACT: J. SMITH

EXHIBIT G
X THEATRICAL

WORKED - W   TEST - T
STARTED - S   HOLD - H
TRAVEL - TR
FINISHED - F W H
REHEARSAL - R S F
MINOR - K R T

CAST	CHARACTER	TR	MAKE-UP HAIR WRDRBE	WORK TIME REPORT ON SET	DSMSS ON SET	DSMSS MU/HAIR WRDRBE	W D M	MEALS 1ST IN	MEAL OUT	2ND N	MEAL OUT	TRAVEL TIME LV. FOR LOC.	ARRIVE ON LOC.	LEAVE LOC.	ARRIVE HOTEL	STUNT ADJUST	M I L E S	M P V	ACTOR'S SIGNATURES
G. JANE	MAGGIE	W	7A	8A	7P		✓	1³⁰	2P		1	6:50A	7A	7P	7:05	—	1		
S. UPTON	VICTOR	W	7A	8A	7P		✓	1³⁰	2P	—	1	6:50A	7A	7P	7P	—	1		
M. RICARDO	BEN	W	7A	8A	7P		✓	1P	2P	—	1	6:50A	7A	7P	7P	—	1		

Approvals:

2nd AD

CO-PROD./UPM

UPM

SAG Sheet

Script Supervisor's Production Report

Film: __TEST DRIVE__   Date: __3-7-97__   Shooting Day: __3__ of __40__

Director: __A. FITZSIMMONS__ D.P.: __D. GARDEN__ Script: __S.N. ZIPP__

Location / Set-Ups	
EKT OPEN ROAD — DAY — MAGGIE + VICTOR FIGHT AS BEN TRIES TO FIX THE CAR LATER THE SAME DAY — THE CAR STILL DOESN'T RUN	Call Time: 7³⁰A First Shot: 8³⁰A 1ˢᵗ Meal: From: 1³⁰P to 2⁰⁰P First Shot: 3P 2ⁿᵈ Meal: From: ___ to ___ Camera Wrap: 7P Credited Scenes: 7, 7B, 11, 13pt - comp

	Script Pages	Script Scenes	Set-Ups	Master Time	Wild Track	Added Scenes	Retake Scenes	Cancel Scenes
Today	2 1/8	4	17	2:00	—	—	—	—
Previous Taken	6	4	37	6:00	—	—	—	—
To Date	8 1/8	8	54	8:00	—	—	—	—
Total Remaining	92 7/8	160	—	88:00	—	—	—	—
Total in Script	101	168	—	96:00	—	—	—	—

Camera Rolls: Sound Rolls: 3, 4

Remarks: A CAM
         B CAM
         STEADICAM

Script Supervisor's Report

WALKIE SIGN OUT SHEET
DEPARTMENT_____

By signing below I agree to make best efforts towards care and maintenance of the equipment .
I understand that all equipment must be returned to production upon completion of assignment.
I agree to notify production immediately of any missing or damaged equipment.

Walkie Number	Accessory	Name	Signature	Date

Walkie-talkie Sign Out Sheet

United States
Film Commissions

ALABAMA
Alabama Film Office
Mr. Michael Boyer
401 Adams Avenue
Montgomery, AL 36104
(800) 633-5898
(205) 242-2077

ALASKA
Alaska Film Office
Ms. Mary Pignalberi
3601 C Street, Suite 700
Anchorage, AK 99503
(907) 562-4163
(907) 563-3575

ARIZONA
Arizona Film Commission
Ms. Linda Peterson Warren
3800 N. Central Avenue
Bldg. D
Phoenix, AZ 85012
(800) 523-6695, (602) 280-1380
(602) 280-1384

City of Phoenix
Motion Picture Office
Ms. Luci Marshall
200 W. Washington, 10th Floor
Phoenix, AZ 85003-1611
(602) 262-4850
(602) 534-2295

Tucson Film Office
Mr. Tom Hilderbrand
32 N. Stone Avenue, Suite 100
Tucson, AZ 895701
(602) 791-4000, (602) 429-1000
(602) 791-4963

ARKANSAS
Arkansas Motion Picture
Development Office
Ms. Suzy Lilly
1 State Capital Mall
Room 2C-200
Little Rock, AR 72201
(501) 682-7676
(501) 682-FILM

CALIFORNIA
California Film Commission
Ms. Patti Stolkin Archuletta
6922 Hollywood Blvd.
Suite 600
Hollywood, CA 90028-6126
(800) 858-4PIX, (213) 736-2465
(213) 736-2522

Entertainment Industry
Development Corp.
Mr. Jonathan Roberts
6922 Hollywood Blvd.
Suite 606
Los Angeles, CA 90028
(213) 957-1000 x3
(213) 463-0613

Orange County Film Office
2 Park Plaza, Suite 100
Irvine, CA 92614
(800) 623-8033
(714)476-0513

Palm Springs Desert Resorts
Convention & Visitors Bureau
Ms. Kim McNulty
69-930 Highway 111, Suite 201
Rancho Mirage, CA 92270
(800) 96-RESORTS
(619) 770-9000
(619) 770-9001

Inland Empire Film
Commission
Ms. Sheri Davis
301 E. Vanderbilt Way
Suite 100
San Bernadino, CA 92408
(800) 500-4367
(909)890-1088

Sacramento Area
Film Commission
Mr. Jan Decker
1421 K Street
Sacramento, CA 95814
(916) 264-7777
(916) 264-7788

San Diego Film Commission
Ms. Cathy Anderson
402 W. Broadway, Suite 1000
San Diego, CA 92101-3585
(619) 234-3456
(619) 234-0571

San Francisco Film & Video
Arts Commission
Ms. Lorrae Rominger
Mayor's Office
401 Van Ness Avenue, #417
San Francisco, CA 94102
(415) 554-6244
(415) 554-6503

San Jose
Film & Video Commission
Mr. Joe O'Kane
333 W. San Carlos, Suite 1000
San Jose, CA 95110
(800) 726-5673, (408) 295-9600
(408) 295-3937

COLORADO
Mayor's Office of Art, Culture
& Film
Mr. Ronald F. Pinkard
280 14th Street
Denver, CO 80202
(303) 640-2686
(303) 640-2737

Colorado Motion Picture &
TV Commission
Mr. Michael Klein
1625 Broadway, Suite 1700
Denver, CO 80202
(303) 620-4500
(303) 620-4545

CONNECTICUT
Connecticut Film, Video &
Media Office
Bert Brown
865 Brook Street
Rocky Hill, CT 06067
(203) 258-4339
(203) 529-0535

DELAWARE
Delaware Film Office
Ms. Carol Myers
99 Kings Highway
P.O. Box 1401
Dover, DE 19903
(800) 441-8846, (302) 739-4271
(302) 739-5749

DISTRICT OF COLUMBIA
Mayor's Office of Motion
Picture & TV
Ms. Crystal Palmer
717 4th Street, N.W., 12th Floor
Washington, DC 20005
(202) 727-6600
(202) 727-3787

FLORIDA
Florida Entertainment
Commission
Mr. John Reitzammer
505 17th Street
Miami Beach, FL 33139
(305) 673-7468
(305) 673-7168

Film & Television Office
Ms. Elizabeth Wentworth
200 E. Las Olas Blvd.
Suite 1850
Ft. Lauderdale, FL 33301
(305) 524-3113
(305)-524-3167

Miami/Dade Office of Film,
TV & Print
Mr. Jeff Peel
111 Northwest 1st Street
Suite 2510
Miami, FL 33128
(305) 375-3288
(305)-375-3266

Metro Orlando Film &
Television Office
Ms. Katherine Ramsberger
200 E. Robinson Street
Suite 600
Orlando, FL 32801
(407) 422-7159
(407) 843-9514

Tampa Film Commission
Ms. Pat Hoyt
111 Madison Street
Suite 1010
Tampa, FL 33602
(813) 223-1111 x 58
(813)229-6616

GEORGIA
Georgia Film &
Videotape Office
Mr. Norman Bielowicz
285 Peachtree Center Avenue,
Suite 1000
Atlanta, GA 30303
(404) 656-3544
(404) 651-9063

HAWAII
Hawaii Film Office
Ms. Georgette Deemer
P.O. Box 2359
Honolulu, HI 96804
(808) 586-2570
(808) 586-2572

Kauai Film Commission
Ms. Judy Drosd
4280-B Rice Street
Lihue, HI 96766
(808) 241-6390
(808) 241-6399

Maui Film Office
Ms. Georja Skinner
200 S. High Street
Wailuku, Maui, HI 96793
(808) 243-7710, (808) 243-7415
(808) 243-7995

Oahu Film Office
Ms. Walea L. Constantinau
530 S. King Street, #306
Honolulu, HI 96813
(808) 527-6108
(808) 523-4666

ILLINOIS
Illinois Film Office
Ron Ver Kuilen
100 W. Randolph, Suite 3-400
Chicago, IL 60601
(312) 814-3600
(312) 814-6175

Chicago Film Office
Mr. Charles Geocaris
1 N. LaSalle, Suite 2165
Chicago, IL 60602
(312) 744-6415
(312) 744-1378

INDIANA
Indiana Film Commission
Ms. Jane Rulon
1 North Capitol, #700
Indianapolis, IN 46204-2288
(317) 232-8829
(317) 233-6887

IOWA
Iowa Film Office
Mr. Wendol M. Jarvis
200 E. Grand Avenue
Des Moines, IA 50309
(515) 242-4726
(515) 242-4859

KANSAS
Kansas Film Commission
Ms. Vicky Henley
700 SW Harrison Street
Suite 1300
Topeka, KS 66603
(913) 296-4927
(913) 296-6988

KENTUCKY
Kentucky Film Commission
Mr. Jim Toole
500 Mero Street
2200 Capitol Plaza Tower
Frankfort, KY 40601
(502) 564-3456
(502) 564-7588

LOUISIANA
Louisiana Film Commission
Mr. Ed Lipscomb
P.O. Box 44320
Baton Rouge, LA 70804-4320
(504) 342-8150
(504) 342-7988

New Orleans Film & Video
Commission
Ms. Kimberly Carbo
1515 Poydras Street
Suite 1200
New Orleans, LA 70112
(504) 565-8104
(504) 565-8108

MARYLAND
Maryland Film Commission
Mr. Michael B. Styer
217 E. Redwood Street
9th Floor
Baltimore, MD 21202
(800) 333-6632, (410) 333-6633
(410) 333-0044

MASSACHUSETTS
Massachusetts Film Office
Robin Dawson
10 Park Plaza, Suite 2310
Boston, MA 02116
(617) 973-8800
(617) 973-8810

Boston Film Office
Ms. Peggy Ings
Boston City Hall, #716
Boston, MA 02201
(617) 635-3245
(617) 635-3031

MICHIGAN
Michigan Film Office
Ms. Janet Lockwood
201 N. Washington Square,
Victor Centre 5th Fl.
Lansing, MI 48913
(517) 373-0638
(517) 373-3872

MINNESOTA
Minnesota Film Board
Mr. Randy Adamsick
Ms. Kelly Pratt
401 N. 3rd Street, Suite 460
Minneapolis, MN 55401
(612) 332-6493
(612) 332-3735

MISSISSIPPI
Mississippi Film Office
Mr. Ward Emling
Box 849
Jackson, MS 39205
(601) 359-3297
(601) 359-5757

MISSOURI
Missouri Film Office
Ms. Sandi Wulff
301 West High, #770
P.O. Box 118
Jefferson City, MO 65102
(314) 751-9050
(314) 751-7384

Kansas City, Missouri
Film Office
Ms. Patti Watkins
10 Petticoat Lane, Suite 250
Kansas City, MO 64106
(816) 221-0636
(816) 221-0189

St. Louis Film Office
Dale E. Lockett, Jr.
330 N. 15th Street
St. Louis, MO 63103
(314) 259-3409, ext. 409
(314) 421-2489

MONTANA
Montana Film Office
Ms. Lonie Stimac
1424 9th Avenue
Helena, MT 59620
(800) 553-4563, (406) 444-2654
(406) 444-1800

NEBRASKA
Nebraska Film Office
Laurie J. Richards
700 S. 16th Street, P.O. Box
9466
Lincoln, NE 68509-4666
(800) 228-4307, (402) 471-3680
(402) 471-3026

NEVADA
Motion Picture Division/
Commission on Economic
Development
Mr. Robert Hirsch
555 E. Washington, Suite 5400
Las Vegas, NV 89101
(702) 486-2711
(702) 486-2712

NEW HAMPSHIRE
New Hampshire Film &
TV Bureau
Ms. Ann Kennard
172 Pembroke Road
P.O. Box 1856
Concord, NH 03302-1856
(603) 271-2598
(603) 271-2629

NEW JERSEY
New Jersey Motion Picture/
TV Commission
Mr. Joseph Friedman
153 Halsey Street
P.O. Box 47023
Newark, NJ 07101
(201) 648-6279
(201) 648-7350

NEW MEXICO
New Mexico Film Office
Ms. Linda Taylor Hutchinson
1050 Old Pecos Trail
Santa Fe, NM 87503
(800) 545-9871, (505) 827-7365
(505) 827-7369

NEW YORK
New York State Governor's
Office/Motion Picture-
TV Development
Ms. Pat Kaufman
633 Third Ave., 33rd Floor
New York, NY 10017
(212) 803-2330
(212) 803-2339

Hudson Valley Film & Video
Office, Inc.
Ms. Diane Kasell
40 Garden Street, 2nd Floor
Poughkeepsie, NY 12601
(914) 473-0318
(914) 473-0082

Mayor's Office Film, Theatre &
Broadcasting
Ms. Patricia Reed Scott
1697 Broadway, 6th Floor
New York, NY 10019
(212) 489-6710
(212) 307-6237

NORTH CAROLINA
North Carolina Film Office
Mr. William Arnold
430 N. Salisbury Street
Raleigh, NC 27611
(800) 232-9227, (919) 733-9900
(919(715-0151

Wilmington Film Office
Mr. Mark Stricklin
1 Estell Lee Place
Wilmington, NC 28401
(910) 762-2611
(910) 762-9765

OHIO
Ohio Film Commission
Ms. Eve Lapolla
77 S. High Street, 29th Floor,
P.O. Box 1001
Columbus, OH 43266-0413
(800) 848-1300, (614) 466-2284
(614) 466-6744

Greater Cincinnati
Film Commission
Ms. Lori Holladay
632 Vine Street, #1010
Cincinnati, OH 45202
(513) 784-1744
(513) 768-8963

Greater Dayton Film
Commission
Ms. Ann Fensel
448 Red Haw Road
Dayton, OH 65405
(513) 277-8090
(513) 277-8090

OKLAHOMA
Oklahoma Film Office
Mr. Robert M. Davis
440 S. Houston, Suite 304
Tulsa, OK 74127-8945
(800) 766-3456, (918) 581-2660
(918) 581-2244

OREGON
Oregon Film & Video Office
Mr. David Woolson
121 SW Salmon Street
Suite 300A
Portland, OR 97204
(503) 229-5832
(503) 229-6869

PENNSYLVANIA
Pennsylvania Film Office
Mr. Timothy D. Chambers
200 N. 3rd Street, Suite 901
Harrisburg, PA 17101
(717) 783-3456
(717)772-3581

Greater Philadelphia
Film Office
Ms. Sharn Pinkenson
1600 Arch Street, 12th Floor
Philadelphia, PA 19103
(215) 686-2668
(215) 686-3659

Pittsburgh Film Office
Ms. Dawn Keezer
Benedum Trees Bldg.
Suite 1300
Pittsburgh, PA 15222
(412) 261-2744
(412) 471-7317

PUERTO RICO
Puerto Rico Film Commission
Manuel A. Biascoechea
355 F.D. Roosevelt Ave.,
Fomento Bldg. #106
San Juan, PR 00918
(809) 758-4747, ext. 2250-57
(809) 756-5706

SOUTH CAROLINA
South Carolina Film Office
Ms. Isabel Hill
P.O. Box 7367
Columbia, SC 29202
(803) 737-0490
(803) 737-3104

SOUTH DAKOTA
South Dakota Film
Commission
Mr. Gary Keller
711 E. Wells Avenue
Pierre, SD 57501-3369
(800) 952-3625, (605) 773-3301
((605) 773-3256

TENNESSEE
Tennessee Film/
Entertainment/
Music Commission
Ms. Marsha Blackburn
320 6th Avenue North
7th Floor
Nashville, TN 37243-0790
(800) 251-8594, (615) 741-3456
(615) 741-5829

Memphis/Shelby County
Film Commission
Ms. Linn Sitler
Beale Street Landing
245 Wagner Place #4
Memphis, TN 38103-3815
(901) 527-8300
(901) 527-8326

Nashville Film Office
Ms. Darrah Meeley
161 4th Avenue North
Nashville, TN 37219
(615) 259-4777
(615) 256-3074

TEXAS
Texas Film Commission
Mr. Tom Copeland
P.O. Box 13246
Austin, TX 78711
(512) 463-9200
(512) 463-4114

Dallas/Fort Worth Regional
Film Commission
Mr. Roger Burke
P.O. Box 610246
DFW Airport, TX 75261
(800) 234-5699, (214) 621-0400
(214) 929-0916

El Paso Film Commission
Ms. Susie Gaines
1 Civic Center Plaza
El Paso, TX 79901
(800) 351-6024, (915) 534-0698
(915) 532-2963

Houston Film Commission
Mr. Rick Ferguson
801 Congress
Houston, TX 77002
(800) 365-7575, (713) 227-3100
(713) 223-3816

San Antonio Film Commission
Ms. Kathy Rhoads
P.O. Box 2277
San Antonio, TX 78230
(800) 447-3372, ext. 730/777,
(210) 270-8700
(210) 270-8782

U.S. VIRGIN ISLANDS
U.S. Virgin Islands Film
Promotion Office
Mr. Manny Centeno
P.O. Box 6400
St. Thomas, V.I. 00804, U.S.V.I.
(809) 775-1444, (809) 774-8784
(809) 774-4390

UTAH
Utah Film Commission
Ms. Leigh von der Esch
324 S. State, Suite 500
Salt Lake City, UT 84114-7330
(800) 453-8824, (801) 538-8740
(801) 538-8886

Park City Film Commission
Ms. Nancy Volmer
P.O. Box 1630
Park City, UT 84060
(800) 453-1360, (801) 649-6100
(801) 649-4132

VIRGINIA
Virginia Film Office
Ms. Marcie Oberndorf-Kelso
901 E. Byrd Street, 19th Floor,
P.O. Box 798
Richmond, VA 23206-0798
(804) 371-8204
(804) 371-8177

WASHINGTON
Washington State Film &
Video Office
Ms. Suzy Kellett
2001 6th Avenue, Suite 2600
Seattle, WA 98121
(206) 464-7148
(206) 464-7222

WEST VIRGINIA
West Virginia Film Office
Mr. Mark McNabb
State Capital, Bldg. 6
Room 525
Charleston, WV 25305-0311
(800) 982-3386, (304) 558-2234
(304) 558-1189

WISCONSIN
Wisconsin Film Office
Mr. Stan Solheim
123 W. Washington Avenue
6th Floor
Madison, WI 53702-0001
(608) 267-3456
(608) 266-3403

City of Milwaukee Film Liaison
Ms. Jennifer Burkel
809 N. Broadway
Milwaukee, WI 53202
(414) 286-5700
(414) 286-5904

WYOMING
Wyoming Film Commission
Mr. Bill Lindstrom
I-25 and College Drive
Cheyenne, WY 82002-0240
(800) 458-6657, (307) 777-7777
(307) 777-6904

Appendix

SCREEN ACTORS GUILD

Arizona
1616 E. Indian School Road,
#330, Phoenix, AZ 85016
602/265-2712

California
235 Pine Street, 11th Floor, San
Francisco, CA 94104
415/391-7510

7827 Convoy Court, Ste. 400,
San Diego, CA 92111
619/278-7695

Colorado**
950 S. Cherry Street, Ste. 502,
Denver, CO 80222
303/757-6226

Florida***
7300 N. Kendall Drive, Miami,
FL 33156
305/670-7677

Georgia
455 E. Paces Ferry Road NE,
Ste. 334, Atlanta, GA 30305
404/239-0131

Hawaii
949 Kapiolani Blvd., Ste. 105,
Honolulu, HI 96814
808/596-0388

Illinois
75 E. Wacker Drive, 14th Floor,
Chicago, IL 60601
312/372-8081

Maryland/Washington, D.C.
The Highland House
5480 Wisconsin Avenue, Ste.
201, Chevy Chase, MD 20815
301/657-2560

Massachusettes
11 Beacon Street, Ste. 515,
Boston, MA 02108
617/742-2688

Michigan
28690 Southfield Road,
Lathrup Village, MI 48076
810/559-9540

Minnesota*
708 N. 1st Street, Ste. 343A,
Minneapolis, MN 55401
612/371-9120

Missouri*
906 Olive Street, Ste. 1006, St.
Louis, MO 63101
314/321-8410

New York
1515 Broadway, 44th Floor,
New York, NY 10036
212/944-1030

Ohio*
1030 Euclid Avenue, Ste. 429,
Cleveland, OH 44115
216/579-9305

Pennsylvania
230 S. Broad Street, 10th Floor,
Philadephia, PA 19102
215/545-3150

Tennessee
1108 17th Avenue South,
Nashville, TN 37212
615/327-2944

Texas
2650 Fountainview, Ste. 326,
Houston, TX 77057
713/972-1806

6060 N. Central Expressway,
Ste. 302-LB 604
Dallas, TX 75206
214/363-8300

Washington*
601 Valley Street, Ste. 200,
Seattle, WA 98109
206/282-2506

AFTRA

6922 Hollywood Blvd., 8th
Floor
Hollywood, CA 90028
213/461-8111

260 Madison Avenue
New York, NY 10016
212/532-0800

EQUITY

New York
165 West 46th Street
New York, NY 10036
212/869-8530

California
6430 Sunset Blvd.
Suite 700
Hollywood, CA 90028
213/462-2334

DIRECTORS GUILD OF AMERICA

California
7920 Sunset Blvd.
Los Angeles, CA 90046
310/289-2000

New York
110 West 57th Street
New York, NY 10019
212/581-0370

Illinois
520 North Michigan Avenue
Suite 1026
Chicago, IL 60611
312/644-5050

CANADA–ACTRA

2239 Young Street, 3rd Floor
Toronto, Ontario
Canada M4S 2B5
415/489-1311
UNION DES ARTISTES (UDA)
416/495-7670

FRANCE– ASSOCIATION DES COMEDIENS ET ARTISTES

40 Rue d'Enghien
75010 Paris, France
47 70 0902
42 02 4224

* AFTRA offices which also handle SAG business for their areas.
** Denver is a regional office which also covers Nevada, New Mexico and Utah
*** Florida is a regional office which also covers Alabama, Arkansas, Louisiana, Mississippi, North Carolina, West Virginia, U.S. Virgin Islands, Puerto Rico and the Caribbean.

Index

About The Author

April Fitzsimmons' production credits as a Set Production Assistant include *Mr. Holland's Opus, Buffalo Girls, Things To Do In Denver When Your Dead, Foxfire, Dunston Checks In, The Phantom* and others. While recently on location in Australia working for noted film director Simon Wincer, April wrote, directed and produced a short film entitled *Polyester Pete*. April is currently working for Gale Anne Hurd who just completed producing *Dante's Peak* and *Virus* for Universal Pictures. April Fitzsimmons spent four years in the Air Force working as an Intelligence Analyst before embarking on a career in the film production business.